Reimbursement Spe

DATABASES • SOFTWARE • EDUCATIONAL PROGRAMS

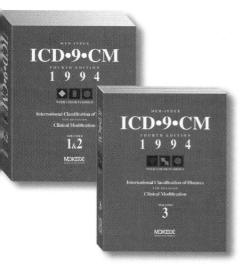

1994 ICD•9, FOURTH EDITION, VOLUMES 1, 2 & 3

NEW COLOR SYMBOLS FOR INSTANT COMPREHENSION

We're confident when we say our *1994 ICD•9* is the best on the market. Under contract with the National Center for Health Statistics, Medicode, Med-Index Division produced the addendum and update material to the *1994 ICD•9, Volumes 1 & 2*. The Health Care Financing Administration has chosen us to produce the official *1994 ICD•9, Volume 3* for the second consecutive year. These contracts mean we can provide you with accurate, high quality ICD•9s.

Medicode also offers new *1994 ICD•9s* with color symbols, developed to improve coding accuracy. Existing color-coded ICD•9s require memorization of more than ten colors; our three color icons simplify the coding process and are easy to remember. Our ICD•9s also include:

• Attachable Quick Tabs™ for easy access to the sections you use most often.

• Definitions for ICD•9 conventions and punctuation.

• Clinical scenarios explaining common coding problems.

• Easy-to-read type printed on high quality paper.

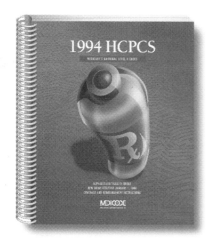

HCPCS 1994

INCLUDES COVERAGE INSTRUCTIONS

HCPCS 1994 is a comprehensive coding reference for durable medical equipment, drugs and select medical services. HCPCS Level II codes are required for Medicare billing and are becoming more widely accepted by private payers.

Medicode's *HCPCS 1994* is easier to use because it includes governing Medicare Carriers Manual and Coverage Issues Manual references that are simplified and placed in one location. Plus, we've cross-referenced the generic drugs listed in the J and K codes to the most frequently prescribed brand name equivalents.

Our detailed table of drugs lists name brands, generic drugs, dosage, route of administration and the correct J or K code. *HCPCS 1994* also teaches you how to bill Level II codes using the HCFA-1500 claim form and clinical training scenarios. *HCPCS 1994* also includes:

• Medicare and Medicaid coverage instructions.

• Cross-references that link deleted HCPCS codes to active codes.

• Complete indexing of all entries for easy lookup.

CPT 1994

INCLUDES NEW CLINICAL EXAMPLES SUPPLEMENT

To help keep up with annual changes in CPT codes, Medicode offers *CPT 1994*, the definitive reference for procedural coding.

The *Clinical Examples Supplement* illustrates scenarios for each Evaluation and Management code.

Choose either the *Medicode Three-Ring Binder*, with a durable, hard cover and easy reference tabs, the spiral bound version with high quality wire-o spine or the softbound version. Many prefer the *Three-Ring Binder* because the book lies flat and is easier to use. The tabs allow you to quickly reference a section.

MED-INDEX DIVISION

Reimbursement Specialists

DATABASES • SOFTWARE • EDUCATIONAL PROGRAMS • PUBLICATIONS

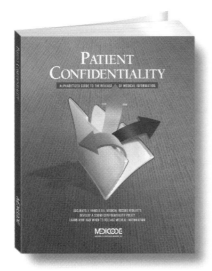

PATIENT CONFIDENTIALITY

RELEASING MEDICAL INFORMATION

Patient Confidentiality is an alphabetized guide to releasing confidential information from your patients' medical records.

Patient Confidentiality describes how to deal with the straight forward as well as the controversial issues. Every topic is covered in clear, nontechnical language. *Patient Confidentiality* also features:

- A guide on how to respond to subpoenas, media inquiries and requests from other physicians.
- AHIMA and ANA approval for 10 CE hours.
- Directions endorsed by AHIMA on releasing information by fax.
- A state-by-state chart listing statutes dealing with medical confidentiality.

By using *Patient Confidentiality*, you'll learn the appropriate, professional way to disclose sensitive information and avoid costly litigation.

CODING ILLUSTRATED

CROSS-REFERENCES CPT, ICD•9 AND HCPCS CODES

Coding Illustrated, the first of its kind, teaches how to accurately use CPT codes through common language descriptions and illustrations. This series also puts CPT, ICD•9 and HCPCS codes together for easy cross-referencing. (ADA codes are cross-referenced when appropriate.)

Coding Illustrated volumes are published by anatomical structure and arranged by CPT code. Easy-to-use tables offer further data on which codes not to bill together, assist-at-surgery, follow-up days and prior approval. Each CPT code is accompanied by detailed illustrations, making it easier for coders to translate operative reports into CPT codes.

Because you only pay for information of specific interest to your practice, *Coding Illustrated* is an excellent and economical resource.

Watch for the following releases:

The Bladder	Sinus & Nasal Mucosa	Uterus Tubes & Ovaries: Nonpregnant
Eye Muscle & Adnexa	The Urethra	Lower Face: Skeletal Structures & Dentition
The Lung	The Breast	Peripheral Vascular System Vol. 1 & 2

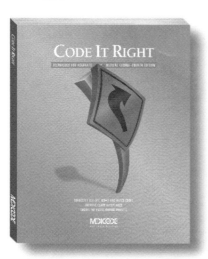

CODE IT RIGHT

REDUCE CLAIM DENIAL AND INCREASE REVENUE

An essential guide to basic coding techniques, *Code It Right, Fourth Edition* teaches ICD•9, CPT and HCPCS Level II coding.

You'll see the whole picture — from clinical service to coding correctly on a HCFA-1500 claim form. And detailed scenarios help you avoid claim denials, audits and revenue loss. *Code It Right* also provides:

- Step-by-step ICD•9 coding with specialty coding for burns, Ob/Gyn, fracture care, mental disorders and others.
- A tutorial to the E/M levels of service and sections on pathology, radiology and surgical services.
- An explanation of the HCPCS coding system for durable medical equipment, drugs and select procedures.

MED-INDEX DIVISION

MEDICAL DOCUMENTATION

STREAMLINING AN ESSENTIAL CLINICAL PROCESS

by Jerry G. Seare, M.D.

DOCUMENT PATIENT RECORDS ACCURATELY AND COMPLETELY
CONSTRUCT LEGALLY SOUND DOCUMENTATION
COMPLY WITH MEDICARE AND PRIVATE PAYER GUIDELINES

MEDICODE

MED-INDEX DIVISION

ISBN 1-56337-079-4

5225 Wiley Post Way, Suite 500
Salt Lake City, UT 84116-2889

About the Author

Jerry G. Seare, M.D., currently serves Medicode as its medical director and as vice president of database development. He has conducted numerous seminars on medical documentation for Medicode's Reimbursement Manager Training Program. He has also conducted chart assessments and audited chart documentation for Medicode's consulting division.

Prior to joining Medicode, Dr. Seare spent time working in the field of biomaterials research at the University of Utah. His efforts were directed toward plastic surgery and nerve repair applications. Additionally, he has served Blue Cross of Southern California as a claims adjudicator.

Dr. Seare holds a bachelor of science degree from the University of Utah, and was awarded his M.D. by the same institution. His clinical experience includes a general surgery residency at the University of Utah Affiliated Hospitals.

Medicode Publishing Staff

Editorial Director   Susan P. Seare

Medical Director   Jerry G. Seare, M.D.

Associate Editor   Lynn Speirs

Project Editor   Marva Bickle

Director of Research and Government Affairs   Barbara Pappadakis

Special thanks to David H. Epperson, Attorney at Law, for his contribution of the chapter on legal issues affecting documentation practices.

Contents

Introduction

Traditionally documentation was generated and used almost solely by physicians as a source of information about patient care. After providing a medical service or performing a surgical procedure, a physician would jot down important information about the patient visit. This information was kept in a patient folder where the physician could easily refer back to it when necessary. The main purpose of documentation was to help the physician remember details of a patient's care weeks, months, or years later.

Up until about 20 years ago, a patient's medical record was seen only by physicians and their staffs. Documentation was not submitted to insurance companies, Medicare did not request copies, and the chances of a medical record becoming a legal document in a malpractice case were small. As a result, standards for recording information were not developed. Physicians could be as detailed or lax in their record keeping as they wanted since often they were the only ones to see the patient's chart.

In the mid 1970s, however, the role of documentation in medicine changed abruptly. The reason for this change was the dramatic increase in medical malpractice claims nationwide. Since many medical liability suits are brought years after the initial care, the physician is not likely to remember all the details. Medical records often provide the main source of information about the patient's care. The patient record thus becomes a legal document that is critical in reconstructing the elements of the patient's medical care. It also can be the only defense a physician has against charges of malpractice.

Medical malpractice was not the only contributing factor to the increased importance of documentation. The Medicare program, created when Congress passed Title XVIII of the Social Security Act in 1966, also played a significant role.

Title XVIII mandates that Medicare pay for services that are medically reasonable and necessary for the diagnosis and treatment of illness and injury as well as for the replacement of malformed or nonfunctioning body parts. But what is medically reasonable and necessary? The medical record holds the key to that determination. In order to determine medical necessity and make sure providers were billing services properly, the Health Care Financing Administration (HCFA), which administers Medicare, began requiring Medicare carriers to perform medical and postpayment review. This type of review involves checking the claims against the documentation after processing and payment to ensure Medicare dollars are being administered correctly.

Computerization added a new dimension to the review process in the 1980s, and claims adjudication became a science rather than a guessing game. Computerized data analysis permitted physician profiling and a more detailed examination of individual physicians, their services, and their billing patterns. What Medicare discovered was that a significant number of physicians and hospitals were billing for services not provided and services not medically reasonable or necessary, costing Medicare millions of dollars each year.

When private payers became aware of Medicare's fraud and abuse findings, they too began to see the importance of verifying that all billed services are actually performed and medically necessary. Although interested, private payers were not reviewing claims aggressively until the outcome of Medicare's mandatory claims review, which began in 1992, was recognized. With the implementation of the Medicare Fee Schedule and the new *Physician's Current Procedural Terminology* (CPT) Evaluation and Management codes, Medicare conducted random claim reviews to verify that physicians were using the new codes correctly. What Medicare found in a high percentage of cases was overcoding (coding to a higher level of service than what was actually provided) and codes that did not match the documentation submitted.

Commercial insurance companies soon realized they also had an immediate financial stake in ensuring that documentation supported all claims submitted. Not only could monitoring claims help them uncover coding mistakes, it was also the first step in getting a handle on the rapidly increasing costs of healthcare. As a result, over the past several years private payers have been randomly auditing claims to verify that the services paid for were actually performed.

With cost-containment strategies in the insurance industry becoming increasingly restrictive, physicians and office staffs need to be aware of the implications of inaccurate or insufficient documentation. As it stands today, incomplete documentation can result in claim denial, even if the denial is due to an oversight as simple as the date of service. From both a legal and reimbursement perspective, failure to document a service rendered translates into nonperformance of the service. To ensure fair and full reimbursement for services performed, the medical record must be documented accurately and completely.

1 Basic Documentation

Proper documentation practices are not only essential for quality patient care, they are also key in ensuring accurate and timely reimbursement. Medicare and private payers will not reimburse an undocumented service and they may delay processing a claim accompanied by incomplete documentation. In addition, good patient record keeping techniques can help protect providers against an unfavorable outcome in a medical malpractice lawsuit. But what constitutes proper documentation and how much documentation is enough? The answer is not a straightforward one. Unfortunately, documentation is not formally taught in medical school, there are no national guidelines, and private payers differ greatly in what they look for in documentation. However, there are some basic guidelines that can be followed to increase the chances for full and fair reimbursement.

Separate Charts

A separate medical chart should be created and maintained for each patient that receives a medical service. Although this is usually standard procedure, occasionally a physician will include documentation for services provided to a child in the parent's medical record when the child is treated during the parent's visit. Physicians should avoid documenting a child's treatment with the parent's because it could potentially create multiple locations for one person's record. At a later date, it may be difficult to locate important information about the child's previous medical care. It can also create problems when copying, forwarding, duplicating, or retiring records.

Permanent Records in Ink

Regardless of whether a medical record ends up in litigation, it is considered a legal document. Therefore, all entries must be made in ink–preferably black ink. Black ink is best because it produces clear, dark writing on photocopies and facsimiles. Pencil and red ink should be avoided altogether because they do not reproduce as well and sometimes not at all. Another reason to avoid pencil is its erasability. Since all entries must remain readable even after a legitimate alteration, there is no reason to use pencil. It may inadvertently arouse suspicion of alteration during litigation involving medical records.

Legible Handwriting

Physicians are notorious for handwriting that even they can't read. However, legible documentation is critical not only in a court of law, but also for proper reimbursement from payers.

Handwriting must be legible to the physician as well as to anyone else who may need to read the patient's chart. As any risk management attorney will tell you, an illegible record is difficult to defend. The importance of this is illustrated by the following scenario.

> A patient with a complicated medical history suffers chest pain and shortness of breath while the physician is out of town. Another physician takes the case in the absence of the patient's usual physician. The new physician is unable to read the patient's chart due to poor handwriting and misunderstands a previous health issue resulting in a bad outcome for the patient. The patient sues both physicians.

Submitting legible documentation to private payers also facilitates correct and timely reimbursement. Private payers are not required to pay a claim accompanied by documentation they cannot read. When confronted with illegible documentation, payers may refuse to pay, or they may send it back and ask for a readable version. With the trend toward more and more documentation review with claims, providing a legible record is crucial for reimbursement.

In summary, the patient's medical record must be legible. If the physician's poor handwriting is due to a busy schedule, then the physician should slow down and write legibly. If the physician's handwriting is illegible regardless of the schedule, then notes should be dictated.

Prompt Entries

Given the busy schedules of most physicians and the number of patients seen each day, it is simply not possible for a physician to remember all details of each patient encounter for any length of time. For that reason, information should be entered in the patient chart at the time of service or immediately following while it is still fresh in the physician's mind. The more time that lapses before information is recorded, the more details that will be lost.

The importance of timely entries is even more critical in cases where the patient is undergoing a complicated set of services in a short period of time by different healthcare providers. The patient's chart becomes a vehicle for communication between the providers regarding the patient's care. If entries are not made at the time of service, crucial information may be missing when another provider needs to refer to the patient's chart. This could have a profoundly negative impact on the patient's medical treatment.

Dictation

Dictation can be an efficient, thorough, and organized method for recording patient information. In fact, more and more physicians are switching from handwritten to dictated notes because they are able to record more information in less time.

However, physicians who dictate their patient notes must take special precautions. Often there is a delay between the patient visit and when the information is placed in the chart. It may even take several days for the transcriptionist to listen to the dictation, transcribe the recorded information, and return it to the physician who must then review it for accuracy, sign it, and place it in the patient's chart. During this lag time, it is important for the physician to place in the chart a summary of the services rendered on that date. The summary must contain enough information about the patient encounter that it could be used in place of the transcription if the transcription is lost, misfiled, or inaccurate. Also, when the transcription is returned, the physician must proof it for accuracy. Any corrections should be made before it becomes part of the record.

Date and Time on All Entries

It may seem obvious that the date and time must accompany all entries, but they are often forgotten during the course of a busy day.

Recording the date of each patient encounter is absolutely critical for the simple reason that the patient chart is a legal document and thus invalid without a date.

Including the time of the service is also important so that the events of a patient's medical treatment can be reconstructed later. Take, for instance, a patient who receives one medical treatment, followed by another event and more medical treatments later on the same date. The time of each treatment must be entered in the patient's chart so that the sequence of events can be established later should it be necessary. If the time of the service is significantly different from the time of the chart entry, both should be recorded in the chart. These steps could be key in preventing a malpractice case.

The amount of time spent with a patient or on a particular procedure can be an important factor under some circumstances. While most CPT codes do not include a time element, there are some codes, such as critical care, preventive medicine counseling, and prolonged physician attendance, that require the physician to record the amount of time spent. Neglecting to document time could result in lost reimbursement dollars, or worse yet, a claim denial.

Also, when documenting time spent providing critical care or prolonged attendance services, always subtract the time spent providing any other billable services. In other words, calculate only the time spent providing critical care or prolonged attendance and not time spent on other services.

Blank Spaces

Information that is recorded in a patient chart should always be entered chronologically. Leaving blank spaces encourages information to be entered out of order. Certain items, such as a patient's previous medical record, may not be available at the time a service is rendered, but may be received by the office soon afterward. In such cases, a written statement should be included in the chart on the date of the service stating that the information is pending. Once the additional information is received and reviewed by the physician, it should be dated and placed in the patient's record chronologically.

Some offices leave blank spaces for the results of laboratory work or x-rays. Once the office receives the results, the staff transfers the information to the blank space. This practice gives the impression that the physician saw the information at the time of the service and thus creates an incorrect and potentially damaging picture of the patient encounter. A better way to handle pending diagnostic information is to make a note in the chart stating that the results are expected. When they are received, date and enter them chronologically. As with all outside information that becomes part of the medical record, the physician should sign or initial the entry to indicate it was seen. This ensures important patient information is not placed in the patient chart without review by the physician.

Title Above Each Entry

Titling each entry in the patient chart may not directly affect patient care, but it does make referencing the material much easier. A title is simply a short description of the purpose of the visit or service placed above the entry. It can consist of one word, in the case of a mammogram, or several words, in the case of an annual physical examination. Some clinics use rubber stamps with the title of the service as well as a space for the date and other important information such as vital signs. Using a stamp can be an efficient way to title entries.

```
┌─────────────────────────────────┐
│     Orthopedic Clinic Visit      │
│   Date _____  │
│                                  │
│   BP_____   HR_____   │
│                                  │
│   T_____  Wt_____    │
└─────────────────────────────────┘
```

If each entry is titled, it is much easier to quickly locate information in the patient chart. It also helps the billing person who scans the chart to spot billable services and makes summarizing the chart more manageable.

Signatures

Payers differ in their signature requirements, but to be safe, obtaining a full signature is the best practice. For Medicare services to be billable, the documentation must be signed. The Health Care Financing Administration (HCFA), which administers Medicare, does not specify whether a full signature is required or whether initials are permitted. Many private payers do not require a signature or initials. But because medical records can and often do become legal documents, a full signature is generally best.

Signatures on Electronic Claims

Last year, HCFA announced plans to require providers to submit Medicare claims electronically with the goal of increasing the percentage of physicians submitting electronic claims to 74 percent by 1994. Private payers are just beginning to use electronic claims submission, but it is likely they will soon catch up.

With the increasing emphasis on electronic billing, it won't be long before the entire process is computerized. In fact, several pilot projects are currently under way to test a completely computerized billing and reimbursement system. In a computerized system, everything related to billing and reimbursement, from claims submission to the medical record, is computerized and transmitted electronically. However, it is not yet clear how signatures would be handled under such a system. Electronic signatures may be acceptable if passwords are used to restrict access.

Cosignatures

Services rendered by a healthcare provider other than the physician may be billable as long as the service is within the scope of the healthcare provider's license and the physician was in the facility at the time of the service. The provider should indicate that the physician was on the premises with a notation such as: "Service directed by Dr. Smith." The nurse, physician assistant, or other healthcare provider must sign the chart entry and the physician must cosign it. Remember, this guideline applies to any person who provides a service that can be billed as ancillary to the physician's service. Each such service must be fully documented in the patient record.

Signatures on Dictation

According to Medicare guidelines, dictated notes must be signed by the physician before they are placed in the patient's chart. A signature alongside the notes indicates the physician read the transcription and approves of the information.

Physicians should not use stamps on dictated notes with statements such as the following: "The information is correct inasmuch as it was transcribed correctly." This statement does not absolve the physician of responsibility for the transcription. The physician must always read and approve of what is transcribed and placed in the patient's chart.

Acronyms and Abbreviations

Standard acronyms that are understood by the general medical community serve as an excellent shorthand tool for physicians. These acronyms are perfectly acceptable in the medical record as long as they are commonly recognized. Physicians should avoid using any personalized or specialty-specific abbreviations. Most hospitals keep a reference list of acceptable acronyms and abbreviations. A list of the most common ones is provided in Appendix A. Also included is a list of several publications on acronyms and abbreviations.

Illustrations

Illustrations are an effective form of medical shorthand. A hand-drawn picture can clearly depict a procedure or describe a finding or symptom in a short period of time. They can also be used to educate the patient or kept in the chart to verify a completed service. What a physician can draw and label in a matter of seconds is often worth paragraphs of information written in the chart.

Two options exist with regard to illustrations: physicians can create the sketches themselves or purchase them commercially. Many commercially available drawings are specialty specific illustrating the areas of the body addressed by a given specialty. Remember that if the illustrations are hand drawn, they must be legible, in ink, dated, and signed. All illustrations used to depict some aspect of a patient encounter must be kept in the chart. (Appendix B contains two tear-out anatomical forms that can be used to illustrate patient encounters.)

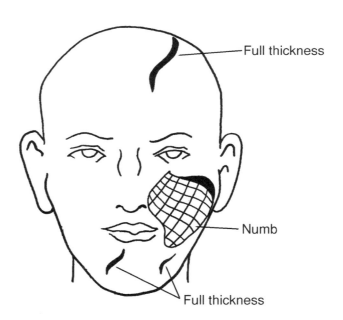

Lesions

When documenting procedures involving lesions, make sure to record the size of each one. If the actual size is not documented, payers will downcode to the smallest size available for that service, which means a lower reimbursement level. CPT reports sizes in metrics so convert inches to centimeters before submitting a claim.

Conversion Chart		
up to 1″	=	up to 2.5 cm
1″ to 2″	=	2.6 to 5.0 cm
2″ to $4^{15}/_{16}$″	=	5.1 cm to 12.6 cm
5″ to $7^{7}/_{8}$″	=	12.6 cm to 20.0 cm
$7^{15}/_{16}$″ to $11^{13}/_{16}$″	=	20.1 cm to 30.0 cm
$11^{13}/_{16}$″	=	30.0 cm

When measuring the size of a lesion, keep the following in mind:

➤ Lacerations and nerve grafts are measured by total length.

➤ Skin grafts and destruction codes are measured by area, calculated by multiplying length by width.

➤ Neoplasms are measured across the biggest dimension.

➤ Tattooing is measured by square centimeters.

➤ Subcutaneous injection of filling material is measured by volume in cubic centimeters.

When dictating operative reports, record the precise size of the affected area even though CPT may not require it. If sizes are recorded, the person reviewing the claim has more information and a better understanding of what was involved in the procedure. This information may support a higher code or use of CPT modifier -22 (unusual procedural services), which can result in higher reimbursement. Remember that recording the precise size involves a mathematical number (2 cm) not just terms like small, medium, or large.

Be aware that HCFA reviews each claim where more than five surgical procedures involving lesion destruction are performed on the same patient on the same day. Some states automatically review claims for more than one lesion destruction per patient per day. Appropriate documentation of lesion destruction consists of the following: diagnosis(es), an anatomic diagram indicating the site(s), size(s), and number(s) of lesions treated, the method of destruction, and any extenuating circumstances.

Skin Grafting

Skin grafting is reported in square centimeters, but burns are often documented by percentage of total body surface area (TBSA) affected. A simple rule for determining the extent of a patient's burn is to remember that the patient's palm is equal to approximately ½ percent of his or her total body surface area. Another method for determining body surface in adults is to use the "Rule of Nines." The total body surface equals 100 percent. Of this:

➤ The head is 9 percent

➤ Each arm is 9 percent

➤ Each side of the trunk (front or back) is 18 percent

➤ Each leg is 18 percent

➤ The perineum is 1 percent

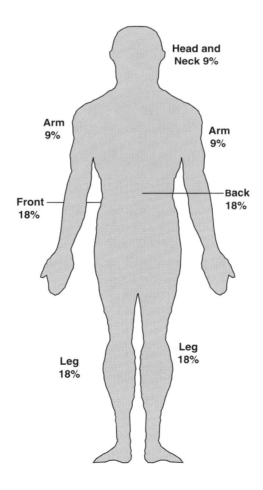

To convert the percentage of TBSA in an adult to square centimeters, multiply the percentage by 2.0 square meters or 20,000 square centimeters.

Changes to the Medical Record

Statistics show that one-third of all medical records involved in litigation have been altered in some way. Risk management attorneys claim they would rather defend a physician with no medical record than one that has been altered. Because there are legitimate reasons for altering a patient's medical record (e.g., inaccurate information that could have an effect on current or future medical decision making), do so carefully and according to some specific guidelines.

When inaccurate information is discovered, the best way to show that it is incorrect is to draw a single line through it. This ensures the information can still be read but does not create the impression the information is being concealed. The physician should then sign and date the alteration. A note citing the location of the correct information should be included for easy reference.

Error. wrong chart. J. Smith 10/19/93. See entry dated 11/17/93.

~~CXR shows left perihilar infiltrate.~~

The correction can then be entered in the patient's chart or attached as an addendum. In addition to adding the new information, the physician should also explain why the information required changing. A reference should be made to the place in the chart where the incorrect information is located. In other words, cross-reference both the incorrect and correct entries.

In cases where information is mistakenly left out of a patient's record, it is acceptable to amend the record. For example, if the results of a patient's lab work are not recorded in the chart at the time they are received, they can and should be added. However, it is important to record the information chronologically by the date the results are actually entered in the chart. They should not be recorded under an earlier date even if they were received earlier.

Another valid reason for altering a patient's record is to document a step accidentally left out of the documentation of a surgical procedure. This is not uncommon especially in complicated surgical procedures involving numerous minor procedures. One acceptable method for dealing with an omission is to include the missing step in an addendum. Another method is for the physician to dictate the entire procedure over again as an addendum. In either case, date and sign the addendum then attach it chronologically. Do not replace the original notes. A note acknowledging the missing information and referencing the addendum should be included with the original notes.

There are times, however, when a patient record should not be altered regardless of the reason. Once a medical record is subpoenaed for possible legal action, it should not be changed. Any alteration can ruin a physician's credibility in court or in front of a jury. To guard against alterations, many hospitals and other healthcare providers collect subpoenaed records and keep them locked up until the legal issue is resolved.

Subjective Judgments

Personal opinion and subjective judgment about the patient or the patient's behavior have no place in the medical record. Patients have the right to request a copy of their records. If that record becomes the subject of a legal dispute, and if it inaccurately portrays the patient, it can be devastating to the physician's defense.

As a matter of habit, patient medical information should be entered in an unemotional and objective manner. For instance, a patient who is slurring, staggering, and smells of alcohol should not be labeled as drunk unless a blood test establishes this fact. Instead describe the patient with objective statements about the way the person speaks, walks, and smells. Certain medical conditions are misleading. Ketoacidosis, which can occur in patients with diabetes, can cause symptoms similar to intoxication.

Also, avoid written and verbal statements that could be misconstrued as a promise of a certain outcome. A sentence like "the patient should see improvement" is an example of something that could be interpreted as a promise. Instead use a more factual statement like "70 percent of patients see improvement." As a rule of thumb, stick to the facts. Do not make statements, whether verbal or in writing, that could be seen as a promise of a certain result.

Documenting a Bad Outcome

Each service rendered by a healthcare provider is done to achieve a specific result. However, because of the many other factors that may come into play, the desired result does not always occur.

Many physicians believe that documenting a bad or less than optimal outcome increases the risk of litigation. This is not necessarily the case. When a bad outcome occurs or when a patient does not respond in the desired way, properly describing it in the documentation is an important way for the physician to demonstrate appropriate management of the treatment. The bad outcome should be documented objectively without any attempt to lay blame or point fingers. The documentation should emphasize how to best deal with or correct the bad outcome. The physician should inform the patient about the outcome and document the conversation in the patient's record. By stating what happened, the physician is not accepting liability. The physician is simply acknowledging the situation and showing an open and honest attitude.

Opinions About Other Physicians

Physicians should avoid writing personal opinions about treatments rendered by other physicians in the patient record. If the patient criticizes another physician, the best way to document the complaint is to write that the patient states the other physician's treatment resulted in a bad outcome.

Referrals

When a patient is referred from one physician to another, it usually falls into one of three categories: consultations, concurrent care (partial transfer of care), or complete transfer of care. Each category involves a unique set of circumstances and special documentation considerations.

Consultations

A consultation involves one physician sending a patient to a second physician for a professional opinion regarding the patient's problem or condition. In order to properly reflect this in the documentation, the requesting physician must state in the patient record that the patient is being sent to a second physician only for an opinion about a particular problem. The second physician may perform a history and exam and conduct any diagnostic tests necessary to provide an opinion. However, the second physician does not assume care of the patient's problem. In order to qualify as a consultation, the intent of the second physician's involvement must be to render an opinion, not to provide treatment.

As much as possible, the requesting physician should avoid using the terms "refer" or "referral" when documenting a consultation. Payers often interpret these words to mean the physician is transferring the patient's care to a second physician. Instead, the requesting physician should state in the record something similar to the following: "I have requested Dr. Warner see this patient in consultation regarding diabetes." The intent in the medical record should be clear that the requesting physician intends to continue to manage the patient's care.

It is appropriate for the consulting physician to order in writing diagnostic services or initiate a treatment plan. The key is that the orders for the treatment plan must be made in writing only. The physician cannot actually carry out the therapy.

For example, an orthopedic surgeon is planning a total knee arthroplasty on a diabetic patient. The physician requests a consultation by an internist for postoperative management of the patient's diabetes. The requesting physician asks the internist to write the initial orders. The internist takes a history, examines the patient, and reviews the records, then makes a final recommendation. The internist records the opinion and writes orders in the patient's chart. Further care of the patient's diabetes is handled by the orthopedic surgeon.

In this scenario, it is clear that by writing the opinion and orders in the chart, the internist is initiating rather than providing therapy.

The consulting physician should also avoid the terms "refer" and "referral" when documenting a consultation. Instead, the consulting physician should state that the patient's physician requested an evaluation of the patient for the purpose of rendering an opinion about a specific problem. The statement must include the name of the physician requesting the consultation and the specific reason for the request.

The consultation should be documented according to the guidelines for documenting evaluation and management services (see Chapter 3, Evaluation and Management Services). Any recommendations should be made in writing.

In addition, the consulting physician should:

➤ Note in the patient record that the patient was sent back to the requesting physician for further care.

➤ Include a statement that all information pertaining to the consultation was sent to the requesting physician in writing. The information must always be provided to the requesting physician in written form. If the problem is acute or serious, it is a good idea to communicate it verbally as well as in writing and indicate it in the medical record.

➤ Avoid stating there will be continued involvement with the patient. A consultation is a single event unless the patient's physician makes another request. However, a single consult may require more than one evaluation of the patient.

➤ Document the consultation directly in the patient chart whenever both physicians have access to the chart. This usually occurs in a hospital or multispecialty clinic setting.

➤ Send a written version of the consultation to the requesting physician if the chart is not readily accessible to both physicians. This usually occurs in the outpatient or office setting.

➤ Initiate therapy only at the request of the patient's attending physician. In other words, the consulting physician should not unilaterally decide to initiate treatment of the patient. If this happens, it is no longer considered a consultation and the service should be coded as a treatment.

Because consultations pay more than concurrent care, some physicians try to make concurrent care seem like a consultation when it is not. Claim reviewers are becoming more astute at detecting this. For that reason, be certain that consultations do not involve actual treatment on the part of the consulting physician. A consultation involves only the services necessary to render an opinion and determine a course of treatment for the patient.

Concurrent Care

If a referral does not qualify as a consultation, it usually falls under concurrent care. Concurrent care involves sending a patient to a second physician for management of a specific problem. It is also considered partial transfer of care. Once the treatment is complete, the patient returns to the care of the first physician. In other words, a small segment of the patient's care is handled by a second physician. The two physicians are thus participating concurrently in the care of the patient.

For example, using the same orthopedic surgeon who is planning a total knee arthroplasty on a diabetic patient, the orthopedic surgeon asks an internist to evaluate and manage the patient's diabetes immediately following the knee surgery. The referral is considered concurrent care because the internist will handle and treat the patient postoperatively for a specified period of time. In this situation, consultation codes should not be used.

Before 1992, CPT contained a concurrent care modifier (-75), which represented care provided by two physicians at the same time. However, there is no longer a CPT mechanism to identify concurrent care. Diagnostic coding, therefore, is extremely important. The documentation and diagnostic coding must reflect the fact that each physician managed a separate medical problem. In the above example, the orthopedic surgeon managed the knee surgery while the internist managed the diabetes. In order to avoid billing problems, each physician involved in concurrent care should only use codes applicable to the problem he or she handled.

This may present some difficulties in cases where two physicians are managing different aspects of the same problem. For example, a cardiothoracic surgeon and cardiologist may simultaneously manage a patient with coronary artery disease. The issue here is that the condition requires the expertise of more than one specialty. In this situation, the diagnostic coding is the same. The documentation, however, should clearly indicate the medical necessity of having more than one specialist involved in the management of the single medical problem. To avoid reimbursement problems, submit a cover letter clearly stating the medical necessity of having two physicians participate in the patient's care.

Transfer of Care

Transfer of care involves transferring medical management of a patient's care to a second physician who assumes complete responsibility for the patient's care permanently or until a specific future date. This category of referral is not usually as confusing as the other two in terms of documentation, but there is one area of concern. When physicians refer a patient to another physician, they should give the patient several names to choose from and note it in the record. If a physician refers a patient to a specific physician and if the patient later sues the second physician for medical malpractice, there may be some overlapping liability because of the referral. If the patient is provided a choice and thus makes the final decision, the referring physician is less liable.

Documentation Checklist

Keeping accurate and thorough patient records is critical to the provider role of furnishing quality healthcare to patients. But also important is the link between good documentation practices and proper reimbursement. The following is a list of the key points described in this chapter that must be addressed in the patient record.

- ➤ Create a single medical record for each patient.
- ➤ Make all entries in black ink.
- ➤ Write legibly. Use drawings, illustrations, and pictures whenever appropriate.
- ➤ Make all entries promptly.
- ➤ Date, time, and sign all entries.
- ➤ Avoid blank spaces in patient records.
- ➤ Document all conversations between the patient and physician and/or staff.
- ➤ Use clear language. Avoid subjective judgment and vague references.
- ➤ Use only standard acronyms and abbreviations.
- ➤ Record all patient interactions including medical visits, conversations, procedures, diagnostic tests, hospital admissions and discharges, telephone calls, etc.

2 Medical Records

The patient's medical record is a compilation of all the information that is gathered and recorded as a result of patient care. The record contains information about the patient's history of illnesses and treatments in a variety of locations, including office, inpatient, and outpatient settings. It also contains opinions and consultations provided by other healthcare providers and ancillary findings such as lab and x-ray results. A well-organized chart that is comprehensive as well as accurate enables the physician to access information quickly and provide quality care.

The medical record is also a legal document, and as such is often subpoenaed as evidence in professional liability claims against healthcare providers. These types of claims have increased significantly during recent years. One way providers can help prevent liability claims is to keep well-documented, organized, and unaltered records, and to maintain clear and effective chart documentation. When malpractice claims do arise, however, a sound medical record is often a physician's best defense.

The basic documentation guidelines discussed in Chapter 1 apply to clinic, office, and hospital charts. This section covers additional issues related to maintaining accurate and complete charts for both inpatient and outpatient visits.

Patient Information

Complete and accurate patient information is an essential component of the medical record. Unfortunately, gathering the information once is not enough. Because people move, change jobs, and switch insurance plans, patient information forms should be updated on a regular basis to avoid delays in claim processing.

Patient information falls into two categories – billing information and medical information. The following two lists show the information that should be gathered for both categories. Remember to keep billing information separate from the patient's medical record.

Patient Billing Information

A patient billing form should collect the following pertinent information:

➤ Patient's full name

➤ Current address and telephone number

➤ Date of birth

➤ Sex

➤ Social security number

➤ Driver's license number

➤ Occupation, employer's name, address, and telephone number

➤ Responsible party (insured), address, and telephone number

➤ Reference: a relative or friend not living with the patient including address and telephone number

➤ Medical insurance information including address, contract or policy number, group number, and effective dates for coverage

Patient Medical Information

A good patient medical information form gathers the following information:

➤ Patient's full name

➤ Current address and telephone number

➤ Date of birth

➤ Sex

➤ Occupation, employer's name, address, and telephone number

➤ Reason for visit

➤ Allergies

➤ Current medications

➤ Previous medical history and pertinent family history

➤ Referring physician name, address, and telephone number

Recording Patient Interactions

Record in the patient chart all interactions between a patient and staff members that could potentially affect the patient's care. This includes not only physician/patient conversations, but also nurse/patient conversations regarding the patient's condition. It can also include less obvious interactions such as the receptionist overhearing a patient express unwillingness to follow the physician's recommended treatment. In this case, what may seen like an innocuous, offhand comment should be recorded because the patient's intent not to follow the physician's instructions has the potential to impact future care.

Telephone calls between the patient and anyone in the office should be recorded. Place message pads visibly at all telephones to encourage staff to note each patient call. Physicians should also keep a message pad by their telephones at home. The messages can then be brought back to the office and transferred in ink to the patient's chart with the date and time of the call and the physician's signature.

```
┌─────────────────────────────────────────────┐
│              Telephone Messages               │
│                                        ☐ AM   │
│  Date _____ Time _____  ☐ PM   │
│                                               │
│  Patient Name _____│
│                                               │
│  Subject _____│
│  _____│
│  _____│
│  _____│
│                                               │
│  Disposition_____ │
│  _____│
│  _____│
│  _____│
│                                               │
│  Physician Signature _____ │
│                                               │
│  Received by _____ │
└─────────────────────────────────────────────┘
```

Document all cancellations and no shows. In a bad outcome case where a patient claims the physician is at fault, the physician will be in a much better position if it can be shown that the patient did not show up for appointments or follow the prescribed course of treatment. Physicians should also record any discussions they have with other physicians about a patient.

Separate Financial and Medical Information

Financial and billing information should not be included in the patient chart. Keeping this information separate from the medical information helps to ensure that the physician's care is not influenced by a patient's financial status. Another reason to separate financial and medical information is to avoid having financial material tied up in litigation should the medical record be subpoenaed.

Loose Papers

With all the components of a patient chart, loose papers can be a problem. If not affixed to the chart, lab work and the results of radiology exams, which are often dropped in the chart after the patient encounter, can easily fall out and get lost in the mountains of paperwork common in most provider settings.

Use a permanent attachment that binds or clips material in the chart to avoid lost patient information. Some offices use tape, others use clips or glue. When the loose papers are smaller than the chart size, affix them to full-size sheets of paper that have adhesive strips.

Remember that all lab slips or outside documents that are to be placed in the patient record should be read, signed, and dated by the physician before they go in the chart. If outside information is not signed, it gives the impression that the physician did not see it and therefore did not take it into consideration in the diagnosis and treatment.

Chart Format

There are a variety of formats that can be used to organize charts. In general, related information should be sorted and filed together. For example, all medical visits should be filed together and kept separate from consultations, lab work, and surgical procedures, each of which should have its own section as well. Once the types of services are organized into sections, they can all be kept together in the chart.

Cross-referencing between the sections may be necessary so that important information in one area that has the potential to impact other areas will be accessible. For example, inpatient procedures must be referenced in the section for medical visits so that any physician who reads that section will be aware of previous surgical procedures. The same reference should be made in all other sections as well.

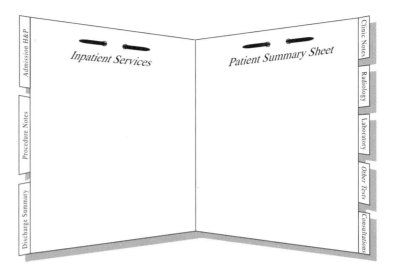

Referencing also applies to other types of patient encounters. If the physician orders an x-ray during a medical visit, a note should be included in the patient chart stating the x-ray was ordered and the date. When the results are received, they should be reviewed by the physician and signed, then labeled, dated, and added to the chart in the section for x-ray results. A note should be made in the section for outpatient visits referencing the results.

Remember to enter all information chronologically reflecting the exact order that the information was reviewed and placed in the chart. It is absolutely critical that the physician review and sign any information that is added to the chart.

SOAP

The SOAP format is a nationally recognized and commonly accepted method of recording patient visits. SOAP is an acronym for Subjective, Objective, Assessment and Plan.

A standard format like SOAP is a valuable way of recording patient encounters in an organized and consistent manner. Without a systematic approach, patient information can turn into a lengthy, rambling, disorganized narrative that varies from physician to physician.

Another benefit of using the SOAP format is that it mirrors the elements of the Evaluation and Management (E/M) levels of service as outlined in CPT. By using the SOAP format, the individual components of an E/M service can be easily recognized in the chart. Coding E/M services thus becomes faster and more straightforward. Chapter 3 covers the SOAP format and coding E/M services in more detail.

Subjective

The subjective portion of the encounter includes all information the patient tells the physician. The physician should make sure that this information includes the patient's chief complaint, a history of the present illness, and a review of the affected systems. Also, the physician should ask about the patient's past history including significant medical, surgical, family, and social factors, and any allergies or medications. The subjective portion of the encounter correlates to the E/M history component.

Objective

The objective portion consists of observed, objective information such as the patient's vital signs and the findings of the physical exam and any diagnostic tests. With the exception of the diagnostic tests, the objective information correlates to the E/M examination component.

Assessment and Plan

The assessment is basically a list of what the physician thinks is wrong with the patient and is best documented by listing one by one the problems, diagnoses, and reasons that led the physician to those diagnoses.

The plan is the further workup or treatment planned for each problem in the assessment list. The plan can be recorded in one of two ways. The physician can list all the problems together, then list separately the plans for the diagnoses. The other method involves listing each problem immediately followed by its plan. Either way, each assessment must have a plan detailing how the problem is to be treated and the final disposition. If there are five problems in the assessment, there should be five problems in the plan.

The assessment and plan aspects of the SOAP format plus the diagnostic tests match the medical decision making component of the E/M levels of service.

Chart Monitoring

Monitoring patient charts should be a dynamic and ongoing activity with one person (if possible) constantly overseeing the entire process making sure that everything the physician ordered was completed.

The charts of patients seen by a physician in the previous month or two should be systematically reviewed checking that the results of any tests or x-rays are back and have been reviewed by the physician and that any dictation has been received, verified, and signed.

The charts of patients who haven't been seen in six months to a year should also be reviewed then filed to inactive. This time period will vary due to the appointment schedules of different providers. In cases where the patient hasn't been seen in more than a year, the file can generally be filed as inactive.

Summary Sheets

As charts become thicker, particularly with long-term patients or patients with significant medical histories, reviewing them before a medical service can be time consuming. To increase efficiency while at the same time preserving access to all important information, a cover sheet summarizing the chart can be placed at the front. Physicians then have a capsulized overview each time the patient is seen.

A good summary sheet is brief but still presents the most important facts. It should include the following information:

➤ Medical allergies

➤ Medications (current and past)

➤ Surgical procedures

➤ Current and past medical diagnoses

➤ Significant diagnostic tests (chest x-ray, EKG, etc.) and results

When starting a new chart for an existing patient, which usually happens when the old one is too large, information from the old chart should be summarized and placed at the front of the new chart. The old information can then be stored and the new chart started with all the important information. Remember that summary sheets must be updated any time important information changes.

Encounter Forms

Encounter forms are strictly an internal tool to transmit information from the physician or medical staff to the billing staff. It is not part of the medical record and therefore not a documentation issue. However, it is important to mention encounter forms briefly at this point.

An encounter form usually consists of a list of CPT codes representing the procedures most commonly performed by the clinic or office. The forms also include patient information and the diagnostic codes relevant to the practice. During the patient encounter, the physician checks off procedures and diagnoses applicable to the patient visit.

Due to the checklist format, encounter forms should not be considered a documentation tool. Coders should rely mainly on the patient record when making coding decisions, although encounter forms can be used as a source of comparison if there are coding problems. To ensure encounter forms are used appropriately, many clinics file them separately.

Because the encounter form is a link between the physician and the billing staff, update it regularly to reflect CPT changes and to include the codes most commonly used by the provider. If an encounter form contains deleted codes or lacks new and updated codes, inaccurate billing is more likely and documentation may not match billed codes.

Fees should not be included on the encounter form to ensure that code selection is not driven by the cost of the service. Price should be filled in later by the billing and reimbursement person. Some offices have computerized systems that automatically generate a price when the code is entered. Either method is acceptable as long as prices are not printed on the encounter form.

Medical Record Checklist

The following is a list of the essential information that should be collected at each patient visit and recorded in the medical record.

- ➤ Patient's name and date of visit
- ➤ Chief complaint or reason for visit
- ➤ Pertinent medical history as appropriate for each visit
- ➤ Vital signs
- ➤ Findings obtained from the physical examination
- ➤ Results of diagnostic tests
- ➤ Diagnostic decisions based on the examination, history, and any applicable test results
- ➤ Indication of progress
- ➤ Medications prescribed with dosage and regimen
- ➤ Notations of consultations or referrals with reason
- ➤ Medical necessity for diagnostic services
- ➤ Treatment plan and rationale
- ➤ Anticipated patient return for further treatment
- ➤ Follow-up instructions to patient
- ➤ Time spent on a visit
- ➤ Documentation of patient education or instruction
- ➤ Signature of physician

Hospital Chart Checklist

Hospital charts have some requirements above and beyond those listed above. The Joint Commission on Accreditation of Healthcare Organizations (JCAHO), which is a national organization that seeks to improve the quality of healthcare provided to the public, has developed guidelines that dictate how hospitals should handle documentation and medical records.

According to the guidelines, inpatient medical records must contain the following:

➤ Patient's name, address, date of birth, and next of kin

➤ Patient's medical history including the chief complaint, details of the present illness, relevant past, social, and family histories and an inventory of body systems

➤ A medical history completed within the first 24 hours of admission to inpatient services

➤ A physical examination completed within 24 hours of admission

➤ A conclusion drawn from the admission history and physical examination

➤ A statement of the course of action planned for the patient while in the hospital

➤ Diagnostic and therapeutic orders

➤ Progress notes made by the medical staff

➤ Consultation reports

➤ Nursing notes and entries by nonphysicians

➤ Reports of procedures, tests, and their results

➤ Reports of pathology and clinical laboratory examinations, radiology and nuclear medicine examinations or treatment

➤ Conclusions at the termination of hospitalization

In addition, JCAHO guidelines require that when there is a transcription or filing delay, a comprehensive operative progress note must be entered in the medical record immediately after surgery to provide pertinent information to anyone attending to the patient.

Each clinical event should be documented as soon as possible after its occurrence. The records of discharged patients must be completed within 30 days following discharge.

Noncompliance with these regulations is taken very seriously by hospitals. Should a doctor consistently fail to keep proper records, most hospitals will take disciplinary actions as severe as the suspension of staff privileges.

3 Evaluation and Management Services

Until just a few years ago, physicians only needed to scribble a few notes about the services they provided and insurance companies would usually pay the fee—no questions asked. But today, as any physician who has undergone a Medicare audit can tell you, the need for accurate and complete documentation is no longer limited to unusual or uncommon services. Routine medical services must also be completely documented in order to meet Medicare and private payer standards.

CPT 1992 unveiled a new set of codes to report medical visit services. Evaluation and Management (E/M) codes now represent 30 percent or more of billed codes. The Health Care Financing Administration (HCFA) is currently considering mandatory national guidelines for documenting E/M services for Medicare. Many physicians are concerned that the guidelines will call for extreme detail, thus adding to the paperwork burden and overhead of the medical office. But regardless of what the new guidelines require, properly and completely documenting a patient visit is a necessity for any practice operating in today's healthcare environment.

Unfortunately, it is not clear what constitutes proper and complete documentation. The degree of documentation required depends on many factors, including the complexity of the service, the specialty of the physician providing it, and the thoroughness of the processor reviewing the claim.

For example, a "normal head and neck exam" means different things to an otolaryngologist (ear, nose, and throat specialist) and an orthopedic surgeon. To complicate matters, claims review is very subjective. In situations where the documentation is borderline, a claim denial or downcoding may be due to the mood of the person reviewing the claim.

As mentioned before, from a legal and reimbursement standpoint, too much documentation is better than not enough. However, documenting every detail of an E/M service is not feasible, or necessary. In general, as long as the service is well substantiated, it is unlikely to be downcoded or denied based on the documentation. Also keep in mind that the higher the level of service billed, the more detailed the documentation must be.

E/M Codes

Coding and billing medical visits involves the use of CPT's E/M codes, which replaced the old level of service codes in 1992. The E/M system encourages good documentation practices because the key components demand greater physician involvement in the coding process and require better clinical knowledge on the part of the coder. The codes are also better keyed to the content of the visit than the previous level of service codes. The result is a more objective coding system.

E/M coding is not without ambiguity, however. Many of the codes prove impractical when applied to patients with numerous medical problems. If the physician addresses all the complaints in the course of a single visit through a mix of problem focused and expanded problem focused histories and exams, directions for code selection point to a lower level. But there are some multiple problem cases that justify a higher level, although this is not explicitly stated anywhere.

Other areas of concern have surfaced as well. Much of the descriptive language lacks the precision that clinicians need when describing a patient encounter. CPT defines a problem focused examination as one that is "limited to the affected body area or organ system." Not only is there a big difference between "body area" and "organ system," but definition of body area can range from one entire side to a very limited anatomical site.

Code Selection

Selecting the right E/M code is dependent on a series of decisions based on components of the service. Each component builds on other components in the progression toward selecting a code. The more detailed the components and the more complex the diagnosis and treatment plan, the higher the level of E/M service.

The E/M components closely resemble the SOAP (Subjective, Objective, Assessment and Plan) approach to clinical evaluations. This is no coincidence. Essentially, E/M coding, like the SOAP method, follows the thinking processes involved in the delivery of a medical service. If the SOAP approach is followed when documenting an E/M service, E/M code selection is much easier. Also, following the SOAP format encourages more complete documentation practices. The elements of the SOAP method are as follows:

S   Subjective — Chief complaint and taking of history

O   Objective — Physical examination and review of data such as x-rays, EKGs, and lab results

A   Assessment — Analysis of problems and working diagnosis(es)

P   Plan — Further workup and treatment

When documenting an E/M service, each element of the SOAP approach should be recorded starting with the patient's chief complaint (usually the presenting problem) and history. Next is the examination and all lab, x-ray and other test results, followed by the assessment and plan. These elements crosswalk to the three key components of an E/M service: history, examination, and medical decision making.

➤   History = Subjective
➤   Examination = Objective
➤   Medical decision making = Assessment and plan

Documenting an E/M Service

The E/M codes are structured according to a common formula: The extent or intensity of select components of a medical encounter, coupled with the risks and complexities associated with the diagnosis and medical decision making determine code selection.

Each E/M service is evaluated on the documentation for that service only. Referring to information obtained during a prior history or examination is not sufficient to allow that information to be included in choosing an E/M level of service for the current service. In other words, each service stands alone.

The documentation must support the level of service chosen for each key component. Medical necessity is the primary factor driving a level of service. Therefore, the severity of the problem being evaluated should directly correspond to the complexity of the level of service chosen. For instance, a minor medical condition in an otherwise healthy patient does not justify Level 5, which is the highest level of service. If complicating circumstances raise the level of service, they must be documented in order to support that higher level.

All three components should be treated independently when assessing the extent of services rendered. The content of each key component is unique to that component and does not apply to the other key components. Never assume that because a history was detailed, the examination was also detailed.

Coders or any other persons reviewing the documentation should not fill in missing information. If a key component is not fully documented for coding and reimbursement purposes, it should be handled as if it was not performed or returned to the physician for further documentation.

Preprinted Forms

Before covering documentation of the three key components in more detail, an important part of the medical visit should be addressed—preprinted forms. Preprinted forms, if used appropriately, can be a fast, efficient way to record a lot of patient information in a short amount of time. Preprinted forms are best suited to the patient history and exam. They are generally not applicable to other elements of the patient encounter such as medical decision making.

Preprinted Patient History Forms

One of the most important elements in a patient's medical record is the health history. Preprinted forms can be a simple, thorough, and quick way to obtain a patient's history. But more important, they ensure that in a busy and hectic office, all important and pertinent questions are asked.

Preprinted forms can be purchased commercially and are usually available by specialty in a fill-in-the-blank format. They can be completed by nurses or other office staff and deal with general patient information such as past medical history and current signs and symptoms.

When using preprinted forms as part of the medical record, the physician must indicate the information was read and taken into consideration. The best way to show this is for the physician to write comments on the form. Comments can pertain to anything abnormal or out of the ordinary, but just as important are any significant normal findings.

The information gathered on preprinted forms can be taken into account in the E/M key components but only if the physician reviews the history with the patient. Time spent obtaining the information cannot be used unless the physician fills out the form. The documentation must show that the physician was actively involved in this process to include time as part of the patient encounter.

Preprinted Patient Exam Forms

Preprinted exam forms are similar in concept to preprinted patient history forms, but have significant drawbacks. Exam forms are available by specialty and usually list anatomical sites with checkoffs for normal or abnormal. The only place for comment is a small blank line or space to explain an abnormal finding.

One pitfall is that because not everything is examined each time a patient is seen, physicians who use these forms often go down the list checking areas as normal that they do not actually examine. Not only does this present incorrect information about the patient exam, it is fraudulent to indicate something was examined when it was not. Also, the patient may have a medical problem but not yet know about it. If the physician checked it "normal" without an actual exam and if the problem is eventually diagnosed, it may be difficult for the physician to explain the normal finding.

The exam form also encourages a less than minimal description of abnormal findings because of space limitations. An abnormal finding cannot be adequately discussed in the space provided on these forms. Whenever abnormal findings are cited, something specific should be said about the nature of the abnormality. Also, significant normal findings should be described, and a checklist tends to prevent this as well.

An alternative to the exam checklist is a form with anatomical headings followed by ample room for the physician to fill in information revealed by the examination. This style of form allows more explanation of the areas checked and forces the physician to write down particulars about the exam. If used properly, these forms can speed up information gathering and encourage completeness, but will not as easily result in recording services that were not rendered.

When using this type of form, avoid statements like "lung exam—normal." Instead note specifically what the lung exam revealed in descriptive, objective terms. This will allow comparisons to be made from one exam to the next and from one doctor to the next.

Also, include in the documentation of a physical a general statement about the overall appearance of the patient. This statement should correlate to the nature of the chief complaint. For example, if the patient is examined for acute respiratory distress, the overall patient condition indicates the patient is experiencing distressed breathing or persistent uncontrollable coughing.

Choosing a Level of E/M Service

When coding a medical visit, the first step is to choose the appropriate level of service for each key component. In order to do this, each of the three components must be evaluated and addressed in the documentation.

Many physicians have resisted using E/M codes because the CPT explanations of the levels of service are not phrased in common physician terminology. However, E/M codes seem to be here to stay and physicians must use them properly in order to receive correct reimbursement.

The following pages describe the three key components – history, examination, and medical decision making – and the subcomponents that must be assessed for each. The key components are described then broken down into levels. For each level, scenarios are provided to illustrate proper documentation practices. These scenarios show how the different levels of each key component should be documented for a chief complaint of cough. Keep in mind that the scenario for the Level 1 history corresponds to the Level 1 examination scenario as well as the Level 1 medical decision making scenario. It may therefore be useful to look at them together for a more complete picture of documentation protocols. The scenarios apply to new and established patients. All levels require a chief complaint (CC).

The Patient History

The history component is categorized by four levels: problem focused, expanded problem focused, detailed, and comprehensive. The levels follow an additive formula, which means each level builds on the previous one. The history component always includes the patient's chief complaint (CC) and a history of the present illness (HPI). The chief complaint should always be a short statement in the patient's own words about the main reason for the visit. The higher levels also include a review of systems (ROS) and past medical history (PMHx), family history (FHx), and social history (SHx).

Level 1: Problem Focused History

A problem focused history is brief and consists of a short description of recent events related to the chief complaint. The history of the present illness does not involve going back in time for in-depth information, and it does not apply to the initial evaluation of chronic problems. Other medical information, such as medications, allergies, and prior surgeries, is not obtained during a problem focused history.

A problem focused history for a new patient usually represents a minor problem that has existed for a short time. For an established patient, a problem focused history only reflects the time that has elapsed since the last evaluation. If little has happened medically, an interval history is appropriate covering only significant information on what has happened since the patient was last evaluated by the physician. An established patient who has been recently ill may have a more complicated interval history, which could support a higher level for the history key component.

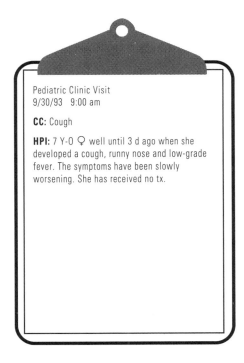

Pediatric Clinic Visit
9/30/93 9:00 am

CC: Cough

HPI: 7 Y-O ♀ well until 3 d ago when she developed a cough, runny nose and low-grade fever. The symptoms have been slowly worsening. She has received no tx.

Level 2: Expanded Problem Focused History

A Level 2 history is described as expanded problem focused. Like Level 1, the history of the chief complaint remains brief, but a problem-pertinent system review is added. This usually requires asking a limited series of focused questions about the involved organ system. It may occasionally involve more than one system.

The problem pertinent system review catches things the patient might have left out. This approach focuses on one aspect of the system rather than a detailed review of the complete system. The purpose is to make sure no additional obvious problems or factors are involved other than what the patient has stated.

Similar to Level 1, the chief complaint is a recent occurrence. However, Level 2 involves a slightly more complex medical condition that requires a limited amount of investigation into associated systems. In this case, an isolated short-term event may be linked to underlying problems and complicated by asthma.

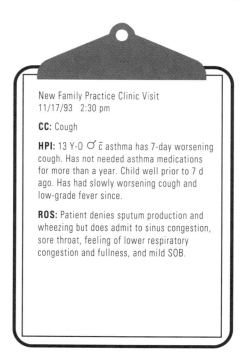

New Family Practice Clinic Visit
11/17/93   2:30 pm

CC: Cough

HPI: 13 Y-O ♂ c̄ asthma has 7-day worsening cough. Has not needed asthma medications for more than a year. Child well prior to 7 d ago. Has had slowly worsening cough and low-grade fever since.

ROS: Patient denies sputum production and wheezing but does admit to sinus congestion, sore throat, feeling of lower respiratory congestion and fullness, and mild SOB.

Level 3: Detailed History

To qualify as a Level 3 history, the physician must take an extended history of the present illness and perform an extended system review. Plus, new elements are added—past medical, family, and social history.

An extended history of the present illness differs from a brief history in that it involves evaluation of a problem that has evolved over time. The physician must go back further and ask the patient about the chain of events that led up to the current problem. The system review, which is now an extended system review, requires asking more questions in greater detail about more than one organ system.

The elements of past medical, family, and social history are added to bring out relevant background information about the patient. The primary purpose is to find out what other medical problems could be associated with or have an impact on the patient's medical condition. Past medical history involves any major medical problems, surgeries, allergies, or medications. It should also include an immunization history and information about childhood illnesses. Family history questions are geared toward the medical problems of blood relatives including siblings, parents, grandparents, and children. The social history seeks information about daily living activities, such as diet, exercise, and smoking, as they relate to the medical problem.

Pulmonary Clinic Visit
10/15/93   10:00 am

CC: Cough

HPI: Pt is 30 Y-O ♀ c̄ 3 wk hx of productive cough. Pt in good health until 3 wk ago when she developed cough. Pt also has fever and SOB. Pt seen in urgent care facility last wk and dx'd c̄ bronchitis and an abx was prescribed. Pt states no improvement p̄ 7 d of abx.

Patient had similar episode 2 y ago. Dx'd as lobar pneumonia and tx'd c̄ abx. Pt has been s̄ pulmonary complaints since that time. Pt states she produces 4 tbsp of viscous green sputum QD.

ROS: Pt denies chronic illnesses and contact c̄ other sick people. She reports she had a ⊖ Tb test 2 y prior and a nl CXR three 3 m ago. She denies night sweats, chills, wt loss, and hemoptysis. She has no cardiac or sinus complaints.

PMHx:
Major med: Lobar pneumonia 2 y prior ⟶ abx.
Surgeries: ∅.
Allergies: NKMA.
Medications: PCN 500 mg PO QID for past 7 d.

FHx: Parents alive, s̄ cardiopulmonary disease.

SHx: 1 ½ PPD tobacco x 3 y, denies exposure to dust, fumes, pets. Works as an accountant.

Level 4: Comprehensive History

The comprehensive history is the highest level and as such should paint a complete picture of the patient's medical condition. In order to warrant this level of service, the nature of the information revealed by the history should point to a serious and/or complicated problem.

Remember that to qualify for a comprehensive level of service, the medical problem may involve one serious problem or multiple, less severe medical problems. For example, managing a patient with hypertension, hypercholesterolemia, and chronic obstructive pulmonary disease (COPD) may justify a comprehensive level of service even without all the specific components of the key elements.

Like the detailed level, the comprehensive level also requires an in-depth review of the patient's history. The difference between the two levels is that the system review is complete. Questions involve all organ systems and a complete past medical, family, and social history. The documentation should show all factors addressed in the history.

Internal Medicine Visit
12/15/93   4:00pm

CC: Cough

HPI: Pt is a 45 Y-O ♂ $\bar{c}$ 6 m hx worsening cough. He was well and $\bar{s}$ complaint until 6 m ago when he developed an occasional, nonproductive cough. This gradually worsened until he began coughing frequently during the day and then recently at night as well. Has tried OTC cough suppressants $\bar{s}$ relief. Also has lost 20 lbs during the past 6 m $\bar{s}$ any change in diet or bowel habits. Has not been previously evaluated or treated for this problem, and has not had any similar problems prior to 6 m ago.

He has mild SOB during exertion. Denies hemoptysis and sputum production. Denies fever and chills. Has a vague sensation of fullness in upper chest. Denies pleuritic pain.

ROS:
Neuro: Denies headaches, dizziness, lightheadedness, numbness and tingling, weakness, fainting.
Skin: Denies rashes, scaling, and any change in moles.
Ears: Denies tinnitus, decreased hearing, earaches, drainage.
Eyes: Denies photophobia, change in vision, double vision, blurred vision.
Nose: Occasional nosebleeds recently, ~ 1 QOD $\bar{s}$ trauma.
Gastrointestinal: Denies dysphagia to solids, has some sense of fullness in throat/chest when swallowing. Denies nausea, vomiting, heartburn, diarrhea, constipation and abdominal pain. Appetite is nl.

Genitourinary: Denies frequency and dysuria. Has nocturia x1. Denies impotence.
Musculoskeletal: Denies joint pain, stiffness, swelling.
Endocrine: Denies flushing, sweating, change in hair or skin texture.
Cardiovascular: Denies chest pain, palpitations, claudication.

PMHx:
Maj Med: Rheumatic fever at age 10. All routine childhood vaccinations. All usual childhood illnesses.
Surgical: Appy at age 16.
Allergies: PCN ⟶ rash, Erythromycin ⟶ N/V.
Medications: ASA $\bar{1}$ PO QD.
Family: Both parents alive. Father-MI at age 62; mother-HTN; four siblings all alive and well; 3 children all $\bar{s}$ medical problems.
Social: Married, accountant, EtOH-∅, tobacco ∅, denies recreational drugs.

The Patient Examination

The examination is the second key component to analyze when determining a level of service. Like the history component, the examination follows the same additive formula and also has the same four levels: problem focused, expanded problem focused, detailed, and comprehensive. A statement regarding the general overall appearance of the patient should be included with any level of exam.

Level 1: Problem Focused Examination

The lowest level of the examination component is the problem focused examination. It is confined to the affected or symptomatic body area or organ system. A problem focused examination involves looking at a very defined or circumscribed part of the body, usually significantly less than a complete organ system. The exam is limited in detail involving only a cursory exam. In the case of a cough, the back of the throat *or* the lungs are briefly examined.

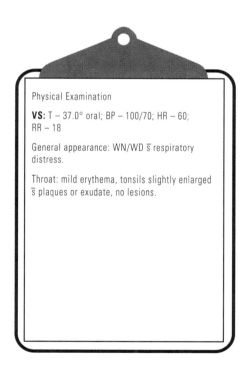

Physical Examination

VS: T – 37.0° oral; BP – 100/70; HR – 60; RR – 18

General appearance: WN/WD s̄ respiratory distress.

Throat: mild erythema, tonsils slightly enlarged s̄ plaques or exudate, no lesions.

Level 2: Expanded Problem Focused Examination

In addition to an examination of the affected area, the expanded problem focused examination includes inspection of a second related or symptomatic area. In the case of a cough, the physician looks at the back of the throat *and* listens to the lungs. The detail of examination for both Levels 1 and 2 is superficial and cursory.

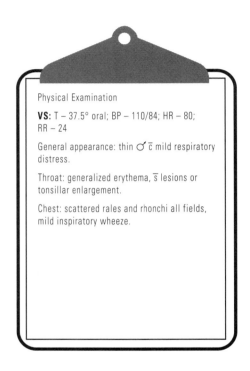

Physical Examination

VS: T – 37.5° oral; BP – 110/84; HR – 80; RR – 24

General appearance: thin ♂ c̄ mild respiratory distress.

Throat: generalized erythema, s̄ lesions or tonsillar enlargement.

Chest: scattered rales and rhonchi all fields, mild inspiratory wheeze.

Level 3: Detailed Examination

Like Levels 1 and 2, the detailed examination encompasses one or more affected areas but in greater detail than the two lower levels. The physical examination for a cough at this level requires looking at the throat and listening to the lungs in detail using more specific examination procedures. The physician may also palpate the neck for signs of swollen lymph nodes or other problems. A more detailed exam of the lungs includes percussion in addition to auscultation. Chest wall motion may be examined and the neck auscultated.

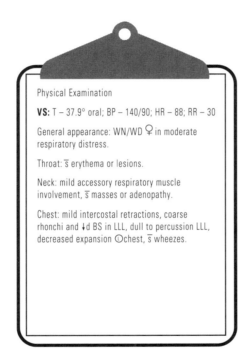

Physical Examination

VS: T – 37.9° oral; BP – 140/90; HR – 88; RR – 30

General appearance: WN/WD ♀ in moderate respiratory distress.

Throat: s̄ erythema or lesions.

Neck: mild accessory respiratory muscle involvement, s̄ masses or adenopathy.

Chest: mild intercostal retractions, coarse rhonchi and ↓d BS in LLL, dull to percussion LLL, decreased expansion ⊙chest, s̄ wheezes.

Level 4: Comprehensive Examination

The comprehensive level includes a complete examination of one or more systems. This level is often confusing to coders because of ambiguity in CPT. The book states that a comprehensive examination can include a complete single system specialty exam or a complete multisystem exam. However, in order for a single system exam to qualify for this level, a specialist would have to look at everything relating to that organ system in great detail and not just the symptomatic area. The specialty exam for a single system would therefore have to include more content than that required for the same system in a multisystem exam.

In the case of a cough, a complete multisystem exam includes detailed examination of the entire cardiorespiratory system including ear, nose, throat, chest, lungs, and heart as well as a survey examination of all other systems.

Physical Examination

VS: T – 36.8° oral; BP – 130/80; HR – 76; RR – 22

General appearance: mildly cachetic ♂, looks older than stated age.

HEENT
Head: NC/AT
Eyes: PERRLA, EOMI, fundi – s̄ lesions, no AV nicking, no papilledema or cupping; sclera – anicteric.
Ears: TMs intact, pearly, s̄ lesions.
Nose: septum midline, s̄ lesions.
Mouth: dentition good, s̄ oral lesions.
Throat: s̄ erythema or lesions.

Neck: supple, s̄ THM, multiple pea-sized (1 cm) hard masses left lower anterior neck – fixed to trachea, s̄ carotid bruit.

Chest: symmetrical unlabored expansion, no retractions, BS slightly↓d LUL, no rales, rhonchi or wheezes, dull to percussion LUL.

Cardiac: PMI @ ☉ ICS, MCL, S$_1$ S$_2$ nl, s̄ RCGM, pulses all 2+ and full all 4 ext.

Abd: soft, scaphoid, nontender, BS ⊕, no HSM, no hernias.

GU: nl ext ♂, testes ↓↓, no masses.

Rectal: prostate soft s̄ masses, tone nl.

Ext: full ROM all 4 ext, s̄ deformity.

Neuro: A&O X 3, CN II ⟶ XII intact.

DTRs

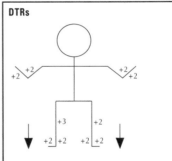

Skin: warm, dry, multiple raised pigmented lesions trunk; nails & hair nl.

Objective Data

Remember that the examination component includes only the physical examination of the patient. Other objective information, such as the results of laboratory tests, x-ray exams, and biopsies, is part of the medical decision making component.

The results of all diagnostic tests should be entered in the chart immediately following the examination. However, since they are part of the medical decision making component, their implications should be assessed there.

When reporting the results of diagnostic tests, the physician should include the date the test was conducted and a summary of the results. For tests the physician reads, such as EKGs or x-rays, indicate that it is the physician's reading rather than a radiologist's or technician's. Create a separate entry for the reading with a reference in the E/M service documentation to the location of the entry. Refer to Chapter 6, Ancillary Services, for more information on documenting diagnostic tests.

Medical Decision Making

Medical decision making is the third and final key component in determining an E/M level of service, and is usually the result of a medical visit. With the addition of objective data, medical decision making mirrors the assessment and plan elements of the SOAP approach to documentation.

There are two ways to document medical decision making in the patient's chart. Both methods are equally acceptable.

1. Assess each of the patient's problems one by one. Then in another entry, list the treatment options for each problem. Using this approach, there will be separate categories for the diagnoses and treatments.

2. List each problem immediately followed by the plan for that problem. This method lists each diagnosis and treatment together.

From a documentation standpoint, all of the patient's active problems should be listed regardless of whether they pertain to the problem in question. A patient that comes in with a cough may need other medical services such as smoking cessation or weight reduction. However, coders must be careful not to consider these when selecting an E/M code and assigning ICD-9 codes unless the problems directly and significantly influence medical decision making.

An important factor in the medical decision making process is comorbidity, which is defined as two separate, unrelated, acute medical problems with two separate treatments, or one acute problem with a complicating underlying chronic illness. In either case, comorbidities can impact the medical management of the patient and should be addressed in the medical decision making. In order for comorbidities to increase the level of service, they must be interrelated or additive, and they must appear in the problem list with an assessment and plan.

Take, for instance, a 53-year-old man with a persistent cough who is a 30-year smoker and works in a coal mine. These factors combine to have a potentially significant impact on the patient's health.

As previously mentioned, the medical decision making component includes an assessment and plan. They are discussed individually below.

Assessment

The assessment should not only discuss the patient's medical problems, it should also review the pertinent history, the significant examination findings, the results of diagnostic tests, and the physician's working diagnosis and rationale. It may also make sense to include a discussion of why the diagnosis could not be a different diagnosis. This often takes the form of a list of rule-out diagnoses. However, if rule-out diagnoses are noted in the documentation, be careful not to use this list when determining ICD-9 codes for the service.

The assessment is an area where physicians have a hard time reaching middle ground—they are either too brief or too wordy. In summary, the assessment should pinpoint the pertinent, most relevant facts.

Plan

For each assessment, there must be a plan, even if it is to do nothing but continue to observe the problem. The plan should also list further diagnostic studies, additional medical evaluations, prescriptions, and recommendations for surgery or other treatments.

An often overlooked aspect of the plan is follow-up care. The plan should include a statement indicating when the physician wants to see the patient again. Avoid using the phrase "patient will return PRN" indicating the patient is to return as needed. This statement is too open-ended. It assumes the patient knows what follow-up treatment is needed and when.

If the patient is under the care of a primary care physician, a return visit should always be scheduled and documented in the medical record even if it is just the patient's next annual checkup. If the patient has been referred to a specialist from another physician, the patient should be referred back at the completion of the specialist's evaluation and a statement to that effect placed in the record.

In addition, the record should always include a list of things the patient is told to watch for that would prompt earlier medical attention than scheduled. This includes specific instructions on how the patient should handle various situations that might arise. For example, "patient told to apply ice pack if area becomes swollen overnight."

Documenting Medical Decision Making

Medical decision making can be the hardest key component to document. Physicians tend to over or under simplify. Plus, coding tends to be subjective because there are no set guidelines as to what constitutes each component at each level. For example, it is not clear how many diagnoses are required to equal the minimal level as opposed to the limited level. The grid below, provides an example of what is required for each level.

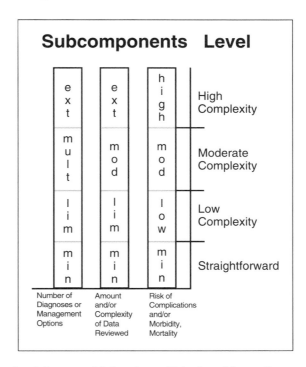

To help coders, physicians could develop a list of problems they most often deal with, then order the list from simple to complex and break it into components of medical decision making. The most simple problem has straightforward decision making, while the most complicated has high complexity.

The following are scenarios for each level in the medical decision making component. Like the other key component scenarios, they are based on the same chief complaint of cough.

Level 1

Assessment
Probable viral URI vs streptococcal sore throat.

Plan
Will obtain throat culture to R/O strep and treat as viral URI. Recheck in one week.

John Smith, M.D.

Level 2

Assessment
Probable mild bronchitis with reactive airway involvement.

Plan
Will do PFTs and begin bronchodilators and oral antibiotic (500 mg PO QID X 14 days). Schedule return visit for 48 hours for recheck. Instructions given to parents to call this office if patient worsens before return visit.

John Smith, M.D.

Level 3

Assessment
1. Productive cough & fever—lung exam consistent with diagnosis of lobar pneumonia.
2. Smoking history.

Plan
1. Obtain chest x-ray to confirm dx of pneumonia. Begin aggressive chest PT. Begin broad spectrum abx 1000 mg IM followed by 500 mg PO QID X 14 days. Recheck in 24 hrs. Instructed patient regarding postural drainage. May need parenteral abx if inadequate response to PO abx.
2. Advised stop smoking and recommended stop smoking program.

John Smith, M.D.

Level 4

Assessment/Plan
1. Chronic cough—history and exam very suspicious for neoplastic process in upper chest/lower neck. History of 20# wt loss also significant in view of unchanged diet. Exam suggests left upper chest process, however, unable to find objective evidence of involvement outside the primary area. Will proceed with CXR followed by CT if ⊕. May need surgical consult for biopsy of neck masses but will wait for results of radiology studies. Will have pt stop ASA use for now in anticipation of surgical procedure. Pt scheduled for return visit in 3 days following radiology study.

John Smith, M.D.

Counseling and Coordination of Care

Counseling and coordination of care are also components of the medical visit, but are less important than the key components of history, examination and medical decision making in terms of choosing a level of service. Since they are not major considerations in most encounters, they generally provide contributory information to the code selection process. The exception is when counseling or coordination of care dominates the encounter (more than 50 percent of the time spent). When this happens, time determines the proper code. Documenting the exact amount of time spent will verify and substantiate the selected code.

Counseling

According to CPT, counseling can involve the patient or the family in order to qualify for reimbursement. Medicare, on the other hand, requires that the patient be physically present to be reimbursable. When documenting counseling, the physician needs to indicate the length of time spent providing counseling as well as the total service time and a summary of the issues and items discussed and who was present.

The following additional items should also be included in the documentation:

- ➤ Discussion of significant medical problems
- ➤ Treatment options
- ➤ Potential risks and benefits of each option
- ➤ Long-term impact of the problem
- ➤ Involvement of other family members and/or care givers
- ➤ Long-term medical arrangements such as home healthcare, nursing home care, etc.

Coordination of Care

When documenting coordination of care, the physician should record the names of any other physicians and healthcare providers involved as well as the amount of time spent and a summary of the discussion including the elements listed previously under counseling.

Summary of E/M Documentation Essentials

The documentation examples provided in this chapter show that each detail of a service need not be documented to be complete. However, significant findings, both positive and negative, need to be recorded. As you look at the examples of acceptable documentation, keep the following things in mind:

Date of Service and Physician Signature

The physician must properly date each service since payers may refuse payment for a service that has no date. The physician must also sign the documentation. While a complete signature is recommended, some payers accept the physician's initials.

Chief Complaint

Every time the patient sees the physician, the patient's reasons for seeking care should be documented. The physician should ask the patient for the chief complaint or reason for service before the history or physical is performed. Note that this is not the same as the presenting problem, which is the underlying disease process resulting in the chief complaint.

History and Exam

The physician should document all significant positive and negative findings. Information regarding the involved organ system but not related to the current problem does not necessarily need to be documented. The physician should demonstrate that a sufficient history was obtained and enough of a physical examination performed to justify the chosen E/M level.

Medical Decision Making

This is the most subjective E/M component and is universally under-documented. Physicians usually just list diagnoses and rarely write down the thought process. The higher the complexity of medical decision making billed for, the more specific the documentation must be. To ensure the level of service billed is justified, physicians need to document the rationale behind their diagnosis and selection of treatment.

Other

Any advice or counseling given to the patient during the course of an encounter should be documented. This includes explaining the diagnosis, the need for further diagnostic services, signs and symptoms to watch for, treatment options with risks and benefits, prescribed and/or dispensed medication including side effects, and specific follow-up arrangements.

Finally, any unusual circumstances of an encounter should be documented. For example, if a patient is brought in by a family member, doesn't speak English, uses a wheelchair, or is uncooperative, it may impact the patient's medical care and therefore should be documented.

4 Surgical Services

Few medical services involve more intricate detail than a complicated surgery. And because the same surgical procedure is often done different ways on different patients, blanket assumptions cannot be made about the way procedures are conducted.

The only visible account of a surgery after completion is the incision site on the patient's body, which rarely reveals clues about the procedure itself. Documentation thus provides the only source of specific information about the surgical procedure and must clearly present exactly how the service was handled in each particular instance. Without sufficient documentation, reconstructing how a procedure was completed at a later date can be extremely difficult. Good documentation practices for surgical services are also important because the details of a prior surgery often impact future surgical procedures.

The importance of documentation is not lost on hospitals. There may not be a physician in practice today who has not received notice from the hospital that dictation is backlogged or unsigned. Hospitals will take drastic steps, maybe even temporarily suspending privileges, to reinforce the importance of physician documentation.

Any procedure that is performed in an operating room with or without a general anesthetic usually requires a formal dictated operative note. An operative report should also be completed for all procedures that warrant a signed patient consent form. Consent forms are discussed in more detail later in this chapter. For more information on the legal issues associated with consent forms, see Chapter 7, Legal Issues.

Minor office procedures or bedside procedures done under a local anesthetic are usually adequately documented by a handwritten chart note. The problem with handwritten notes is that they tend to be less complete and harder to read than dictated notes. So when writing notes by hand, make sure they are legible and contain the level of detail required by the type of procedure performed.

Operative reports, also known as procedural notes, should follow the basic documentation guidelines discussed in Chapter 1. This chapter highlights some additional issues specific to operative reports.

Dictation

While dictation can be a speedier and more efficient way to document operative reports, it does require certain precautions to ensure the patient record is complete at all times. In a busy hospital, dictation can backlog causing a few days to lapse between the time the dictation is submitted to the transcriptionist and when it is returned, read, and signed by the physician then placed in the patient's chart. A brief handwritten summary of the procedure should always be kept in the patient's record until the dictation returns from the transcriptionist. This ensures that important information about the patient's care is immediately available.

Do not be misled by the word summary. The summary must contain enough information about the surgical procedure that it could be used to recreate the operative report in the event the transcription is lost. In addition to the basic elements such as date, signature, and time, the summary and complete operative report should contain the following items:

➤ Pre- and postoperative diagnoses
➤ Title of procedure
➤ Surgeon, cosurgeon, assistant surgeon
➤ Anesthetic and anesthesiologist
➤ Summary of procedure
➤ Complications and unusual services
➤ Immediate postoperative condition
➤ Estimate of blood loss and replacement
➤ Fluids given and invasive tubes, drains, and catheters used

While all elements may not be necessary on every report, their importance increases with the complexity of the procedure. A biopsy, for example, does not require the same level of detail as an open laparotomy procedure.

Elements of the Operative Report

Preoperative Diagnosis

The preoperative diagnosis is often a presumed diagnosis as findings during and after surgery can lead to a different postoperative diagnosis.

Postoperative Diagnosis

The postoperative diagnosis may be a more definitive diagnosis based on intraoperative findings. This diagnosis is the basis for ICD-9 code selection.

Title of Procedure

Include a listing of all procedures performed, usually in chronological order. If eponyms are used, add a technical description to ensure proper understanding by anyone else who may see the chart. When cosurgeons are involved, include the titles of the procedures each performed. Procedures performed by the anesthesiologist are also usually listed here.

Surgeons

All surgeons involved with the procedure should be listed, including the primary surgeon and any cosurgeons and assistant surgeons.

For surgical procedures with more than one surgeon, the primary surgeon is responsible for the procedural note. A resident, intern, or assistant can dictate the note, but the primary surgeon must indicate agreement by reading and signing it.

Do not confuse cosurgeons with assistant surgeons. Cosurgeons, usually called in to handle a particular area of expertise, have shared responsibility in the procedure and must record their involvement. Assistant surgeons, on the other hand, only provide assistance when needed. They do not have their own responsibilities and therefore do not dictate any part of the note.

When cosurgeons dictate a portion of the procedure, they should make clear at what point they became involved. The following statement is a good way to communicate this: "Dr. Green performed an abdominal hysterectomy. I then proceeded with a resection of the rectum and colon and a colostomy. After finishing, I turned it over to Dr. White, who removed the bladder and transplanted the ureters."

Due to the complex nature of some surgeries requiring the expertise of several cosurgeons, the dictation can become quite complicated. The best way to handle such a situation is for one of the surgeons to be placed in charge of the overall dictation. That surgeon then gives an overview of the entire procedure describing each surgeon's role and where that role fits into the procedure as a whole. Each surgeon then dictates his or her involvement using the procedure in detail format.

Anesthesia and Anesthesiologist

The type of anesthesia used should be reported with the name of the anesthesiologist or nurse anesthetist. It is often helpful to note the anesthesia time as well.

Indications

Noting indications helps establish the medical necessity of the procedure. Include a brief history or summary of what caused the patient to need the surgical procedure.

Summary of Findings at Surgery

The findings at surgery must be completely documented. Report all findings pertinent to the procedure, whether normal or abnormal. Normal findings that do not relate to the current problem are unnecessary. A more detailed account of all findings is usually included in the procedure detail.

Procedure in Detail

The procedure in detail constitutes the ultimate source of documentation for the procedure, and payers consider it the final resource for payment decisions. It should read like a step-by-step report of the operation and be as descriptive as possible using phrases that reflect CPT terminology to aid proper coding. Include the structures and layers of tissue involved as well as the length of all incisions and the size of all pertinent normal or abnormal structures. The bottom line is: If it isn't found here, it may not be reimbursable.

These detailed descriptions require careful documentation practices. Cutting corners in an effort to save time can compromise the quality of the description. For example, some physicians document commonly performed procedures in the following way: "Performed hysterectomy in usual fashion." Avoid such ambiguous statements in the documentation because it assumes there is a national standard that guides how the procedure should be performed. A physician in a different area may wonder if specific components of the "usual" procedure were included or omitted. Since there are many ways to perform almost any procedure, a physician in Montana may not have the same concept of "usual" as a physician in Florida.

Similarly, do not assume that eponyms are sufficient to describe a procedure. For example: "Completed MMK in usual fashion" is a common notation referring to the Marshall-Marchetti-Krantz method of performing a urethrocystopexy. The problem is that eponyms do not provide sufficient information about the procedure and how it was performed. Instead, the description should include a report of any abnormalities or special circumstances, and most importantly, any complications or differences in approach. Be detailed when documenting such things as size of structure, pathology, sutures, unusual anatomy, and so on.

When reporting complications, document the nature of the complication as well as the amount of time the physician spent dealing with it in relation to the overall length of the surgery. If one hour of a nine-hour surgery was spent dissecting adhesions, state that fact in the documentation. Not only will this practice make the documentation more complete and accurate, it is necessary to support a higher level of coding. Using key words like difficult, complicated, or unusual in the documentation can also help reflect a higher level.

Complications

Any intraoperative misadventure should be summarized in the complications section of the operative report. Specific information about the complication and the steps taken to deal with it belong in the procedure in detail section.

In addition, record any complications that result in a negative effect on the patient. Avoid speculating on the future impact of a complication. Instead, comment on any immediate observable effects on the patient.

Some physicians feel that documenting a complication, unusual situation, or misadventure that does not result in a bad patient outcome only increases the risk of a malpractice suit. However, attorneys agree that not reporting these problems raises suspicion in the event of a lawsuit.

Unusual Services

Any time a procedure involves services that are unusual or unique, document them carefully in the patient record and include an explanation of why the procedure was unusual. For instance, did it involve dissecting extensive adhesions or was unusual anatomy discovered? Also, describe the action taken to deal with the unusual circumstance and how much time was spent. If the unusual circumstance involved a nonstandard approach or some other unique way of accomplishing the procedure, that information should be reported as well.

Document unusual circumstances encountered during the procedure factually. Avoid commenting on the future implications of the unusual circumstance, instead objectively describe the problem and how it was handled. Physicians often try to leave themselves a back door by saying in advance the patient may experience a slower than usual recovery due to the unusual event. Because the patient record is a factual account, make no such statement unless the patient does experience slow or less than optimal healing.

When dictating unusual services, the physician should state that the procedure was unusual and explain how it compares to the same procedure under normal circumstances. Document unusual instruments, such as microscopes or video cameras, used during a procedure.

Postoperative Condition

The condition of the patient at the completion of the surgery as well as the disposition (postoperative location of the patient) should be documented in the operative report, whether the patient is stable in a recovery room or critical in the intensive care unit.

Additional Information

The following elements should also be included in the documentation where applicable: estimated blood loss (compared to the normal range), type and quantity of intraoperative fluids given including blood, and any catheters, tubes, or drains left in the patient including intravenous blood lines, arterial lines, urinary catheters, endotracheal tubes, or drainage systems left in the operative area. Also, note any foreign bodies intentionally left hidden in the operative site.

Do not forget to note that sponge, needle, and instrument counts were made and the result. If a sponge or instrument is intentionally left in the surgical site, indicate it here along with the reason and plan for future removal.

Alternative Therapies

With the increasing medical/legal liabilities involved in operative procedures, it is important to indicate that the patient was given adequate information to make an informed consent, including information on alternative therapies.

Don't be surprised if patients request information on alternative therapies. Now more than ever people want to know about any and all available alternatives to surgery. The operative report should contain a note stating that alternative therapies were discussed with the patient and the risks and benefits associated with those therapies as well as the risks and benefits of surgery. Make sure the alternative therapies are individually named in the operative report and state the risks and benefits of each one along with a statement outlining the risks and benefits of the current surgery. The physician should note that the patient indicated an understanding of the discussion.

The patient's final choice of treatment should also be documented in the record. While this is part of the consent form that each patient signs before undergoing a surgical procedure, it is a good idea to note it in the operative report as well.

Indicate also that the identity of the patient was verified as well as the operative site (e.g., right or left side if performing a hernia repair). Some surgeons have their patients mark the site themselves and add it to the report. Finally, note the method of transportation to the operating room and the patient's status during transport. For example, "Pt transported by gurney to OR after IV sedation."

Read Before Signing

As with other types of services, if dictation is the method used to document an operative report, the surgeon must read the transcription before signing it. Dictation commonly contains words that might not be easy for a transcriptionist to hear clearly. The transcription, therefore, may contain inaccuracies and spelling errors. To ensure this does not become part of the patient's permanent medical record, the physician must read the transcription completely before signing. The transcription is not technically official until signed, so changes can easily be made up to that point. A copy should also go into the patient's clinic chart so that two separate copies are maintained making cross-referencing easier.

Dictation should be completed as soon as possible after the procedure. The longer the time that lapses, the greater the chance that important details will be lost.

Although it is preferable for the primary surgeon to dictate the report, it is occasionally done by an assistant or resident. When this happens, the primary surgeon must be highly involved in the process. The physician should carefully read the report to make sure nothing is missing and actively monitor it for statements about unusual procedures. After all, the surgeon is the one responsible for the documentation and accountable in a court of law.

Preprinted Operative Report Forms

Some surgeons have developed preprinted operative reports with blanks left for information specific to the patient. The rationale is that a surgeon performs common surgical procedures the same way most of the time. The problem is the tendency to use the same form even when the procedure is different or unusual and not make alterations to reflect those differences. For that reason, preprinted operative report forms may encourage inflexibility and should be avoided for anything but the most simple procedures.

A template that guides the layout and provides room for discussion of the general issues is an acceptable alternative. Another alternative is to use a preprinted operative report form as a script to dictate from, or to use when adding or changing information contained in the dictation. These alternatives help avoid being locked into a printed format that may be unsuitable for every situation and cannot be easily changed.

Consent

Technically, every medical service requires some type of patient consent. Routine office visits fall into the category of implied consent, which means the patient has automatically agreed to a certain level of treatment by making an appointment and presenting in the physician's office. Invasive procedures, which involve breaking and entering the skin or body cavity with an instrument, usually require written consent.

However, not every procedure that involves breaking and entering the skin with an instrument requires written consent. For example, when drawing blood, the skin is penetrated by a needle. But in most cases, drawing blood does not require a written consent.

In general, two factors determine that a procedure requires written consent. The procedure must be invasive or carry significant risk, and the treatment must have an alternative. Life-saving emergency procedures do not usually require consent because there is no alternative. Most procedures, however, are not emergencies and have alternatives.

As with many aspects of documentation, there are gray areas surrounding the issue of consent. Some procedures obviously need a written consent, while others obviously do not. A good rule of thumb is that if the physician wonders whether to obtain a patient's consent, then it is probably a good idea to request one. It is never inappropriate to ask for one.

Some physicians never obtain a signed consent. Many of these physicians believe there is no true informed consent because people cannot know enough about the risks involved and the treatment options without formal medical training. They think consent forms are useless legally because consent cannot truly be informed consent. While this argument has some merit, consent should still be obtained for invasive procedures that carry risk. Physicians who do not obtain consent risk assault charges. A carefully worded and properly obtained consent is unlikely to be used successfully against the physician in a malpractice action.

When discussing a proposed surgical procedure with a patient, the physician should include a description of the procedure, the expected benefit and inherent risks, and the alternative treatments along with their risks and benefits. Consent should be obtained as close to the time of the procedure as possible. Avoid obtaining consent months ahead of time.

The following items should be included in a written consent:

➤ The procedure title in medical terms and lay terms. For example, "Cholecystectomy (surgical removal of the gallbladder)."

➤ A sentence stating alternative therapies were discussed with the patient. The alternatives should be listed along with their risks and benefits.

➤ A discussion of the procedure's potential complications and anticipated outcome should be reflected on the consent including the following: risks (infection, bleeding, or death), likelihood of risks, and anticipated outcome. (Indicate the anticipated outcome, but be careful that it is not construed as a guarantee of a certain result.)

➤ A statement indicating the above items were discussed with the patient and the patient understood them and wishes to go ahead with the procedure

➤ Patient signature

➤ Witness signature

➤ Date and time

Preprinted Consent Forms

Preprinted consent forms are available commercially and usually come in a fill-in-the-blank format. Although they are better than no consent form at all, they have their limitations. Fill-in-the-blank forms do not allow for a detailed description of the issues discussed with the patient. Should the patient's consent ever become an issue in a legal case, a consent form that encourages detail will have greater impact than a generic fill-in-the-blank form.

There are two extremes with regard to consent forms. Many hospitals and physicians use preprinted consent forms that are brief, filled out by a nurse, and signed in admissions. At the other end of the spectrum are physicians who ask their patients to hand write their consent in the chart with a summary of all the issues discussed. Both extremes leave out the crucial role of the physician. Consent should be handled by the physician, not by the patient and not by the admitting staff.

Consent for Anesthesia

When anesthesia other than a local is used, a separate consent is required covering the same elements as the surgical consent. Include the proposed anesthesia and the risks and benefits as well as any alternatives and the risks and benefits of each alternative. The patient must also sign the consent.

Operative Report Checklist

The following is a list of the information that should be gathered and included in the operative report.

➤ Date and time of procedure

➤ Medical necessity of the procedure for the treatment of the patient's condition (preoperative diagnosis)

➤ Summary of the procedures performed and techniques used

➤ Patient preparation including cleansing, medications, enemas, anesthesia, etc.

➤ Medications used

➤ Instruments and/or machinery used

➤ Depth and extent of incisions

➤ Clinical findings during the procedure

➤ Nature, location, and depth of injections

➤ Depth of instrument penetrations through body orifices or cavities

➤ Foreign bodies observed or removed

➤ Nature and amount of material drained

➤ Location, number, and size of lesions excised, biopsied, curetted, frozen, exposed to laser light, or otherwise removed

➤ Nature, source, and size of specimens sent for pathological examination (results of pathological examinations must be incorporated into the patient's medical record when they are received)

➤ Reference to any appliances, hardware, etc. left in patient

➤ Means of wound closure or dressing

➤ Patient's condition at the end of the procedure

➤ Instructions for care after the procedure

➤ Postoperative diagnosis(es)

➤ Name and signature of primary surgeon and the names of any surgical assistants

➤ Legible and detailed description of procedure allowing another health professional reading the report to understand the nature and extent of the procedure

➤ For complicated procedures, the length of the procedure, full documentation of anesthesia provided, and the names of any surgical assistants and the nature and extent of their participation

Nonphysician Services

Physicians are not the only ones who provide medical care to patients. Many medical services are provided by nonphysicians such as registered nurses, physician assistants, nurse practitioners, certified registered nurse anesthetists, and registered physical therapists. All are licensed to provide specific services under the supervision or direction of a physician. While the care they provide is usually in conjunction with the physician's service, there are instances when nonphysician practitioners act independently. In either case, the documentation requirements for nonphysicians are the same as those for physicians, with the addition of information concerning the physician's role in directing or supervising care.

When documenting nonphysician services, the physician should note the need for and level of involvement of the nonphysician provider. Also record the level of supervision provided. Many services require direct physician involvement in order to be billable. Other services only require a referral from a physician. It is important to know the specific requirements and indicate in the medical record the appropriate level of participation.

In general, private payers reimburse services rendered by nonphysicans as long as they are provided in conjunction with the physician's services. Reimbursement is usually handled by combining and billing the nonphysician's services with the physician's services. In some instances, nonphysicians may bill their services separately.

Medicare also allows payment for nonphysician services. Some nonphysician services require indirect supervision while others require direct supervision. Locality and the type of service provided determine the appropriate level of physician supervision, and the documentation must reference the level of supervision.

Resident Services

Payment may be made for a physician's fees as long as the physician qualifies as an attending physician and is physically present when the resident performs the service. Medicare payment is the same whether the physician performs the service or the resident performs the service in the presence of the attending physician. A service furnished by a resident without the presence of the attending physician is not covered under Medicare.

Each time a resident makes an entry in a patient chart, whether for an E/M service or a procedure, the record must be cosigned by the supervising physician to indicate that the resident is participating in the care of the patient under the direct supervision of an attending physician. All billable services require documentation by the attending physician.

Private Payers and Resident Services

Private payers have a different policy on resident services. Most feel that because residents are medical doctors after their first year of internship and have a state license, they must be reimbursed for their services. The resident's documentation must meet the same criteria as a practicing physician's documentation. Check local and state regulations and residency program guidelines prior to billing services.

5 Ancillary Services

Documenting Radiology Services

Over the past few years, payers have significantly increased their scrutiny of radiology services. As a result, payment for radiological exams that are not shown to be medically necessary are often denied by payers. Diagnostic coding is critical in establishing medical necessity. However, the radiologist is frequently not given enough information by the referring physician to assign an appropriate diagnostic code. For example, many radiological services are performed to rule out a particular problem. When these tests are normal, the radiologist often does not know enough about patient's clinical history to justify the reimbursement.

In general, when a patient undergoes a radiological exam, the patient's physician orders the study and a radiologist performs and/or interprets the procedure. The radiologist then sends a report back to the referring physician who summarizes the report and includes it in the overall assessment of the patient. For coding and reimbursement purposes, the radiologist bills the supervision and interpretation of the study. The ordering physician evaluates the results of the study for consideration in the medical decision making but does not bill any portion of the radiological study.

When documenting radiological services, there are two aspects to consider: the attending (requesting) physician's responsibilities and the radiologist's responsibilities.

Requesting Physician Responsibilities

With the current increased emphasis on the medical necessity of radiological services, the radiologist must be informed about the reason for the exam. It is the responsibility of the ordering physician or other person ordering the study to provide this information. Remember that even routine radiological studies, such as x-rays for preoperative clearance or for family history, personal history, or environmental factors, must be medically necessary.

When the results come in from the radiologist, the physician should sign all reports as evidence the information was reviewed and taken into consideration in the medical decision making. While the actual film is generally stored elsewhere, a written report should be incorporated into the patient's medical record in the event the physician should ever need to prove the study was medically necessary.

Radiologist Responsibilities

Radiologists must complete a report on every service they bill following the same basic guidelines discussed in Chapter 1. The specific name or title of the study should appear at the top of the report; for example, "Chest x-ray, PA and lateral."

In addition to reporting the number and type of views taken, reports must also indicate any special circumstances that may affect the exam. For example, a patient's state of fasting for a bowel study can potentially impact the study. In addition to the above elements, documentation of a radiological exam should also include:

- ➤ Quality of the study (clear or blurry)
- ➤ Pertinent positive findings (abnormal)
- ➤ Pertinent negative findings (normal)
- ➤ Other aspects of the film such as incidental findings in other areas
- ➤ Radiologist's impression and diagnosis
- ➤ Recommendations for further studies or treatment
- ➤ Signature

Radiology reports are almost universally transcribed. For that reason, some special precautions must be taken to ensure the patient record is kept current. Whenever possible, apply the rules for dictated operative reports to radiology reports (see Chapter 4, Surgical Services). For example, place a handwritten summary of the study in the chart until the transcription is available. The radiologist must read the transcription for accuracy and sign it before it is sent to the ordering physician or placed permanently in the patient's record.

In addition to the number and type of views taken, dictated reports should also include whether the study required a contrast medium, the type and amount of contrast medium or radionuclide, and other pertinent information relative to the procedure. This information is necessary to support CPT code selection and alleviate any additional time necessary for verification. It will also aid in more timely reimbursement when documentation is requested by a third party payer.

The following list identifies different types of radiology services and the key elements that should be documented to support the complexity of the procedure:

➤ Diagnostic procedures
- number of views
- limited or complete
- unilateral or bilateral
- with or without KUB
- with or without contrast media (type and amount)

➤ Ultrasound procedures and noninvasive vascular diagnostic studies (NVDS)
- complete or limited/follow-up
- unilateral or bilateral
- with or without duplex scan

➤ Nuclear medicine procedures
- type and amount of radionuclide
- limited, multiple area, or whole body
- single or multiple determination
- with or without flow
- qualitative or quantitative

➤ Computed tomography (CT)
- with or without contrast media (type and amount)
- multiplanar scanning and/or reconstruction

➤ Magnetic resonance imaging (MRI)
- with or without contrast media (type and amount)
- number of sequences

If extra views are performed in addition to what is usual for a given study, they should be carefully noted in the documentation. The exam may qualify for additional reimbursement when CPT modifier -22 (unusual procedural services) is added to the CPT code.

Even though the physician must indicate the medical necessity when ordering a radiological study, the radiologist must also briefly indicate the reason in the report. The more complicated the study, the more in-depth the statement should be.

When radiological studies are done for urgent, acute problems, the results must be communicated verbally by the radiologist to the physician as soon as they are available. In these cases, the outcome of the study is often crucial to the physician's diagnosis and treatment. These conversations must be documented in the patient record.

Second Readings

A radiological study is sometimes interpreted again by the requesting physician after the radiologist's interpretation. A second interpretation cannot be billed because it is considered part of the overall patient assessment.

If the physician disagrees with the radiologist's findings, it should not be recorded in the patient chart. A patient's medical record should not be a forum for debate between two physicians. If the patient's record ever becomes the subject of a medical malpractice claim, such disagreements are hard to defend before a jury. The physician should discuss any differences of opinion with the radiologist and if a change in interpretation is made, enter a final corrected impression in the chart including a brief note stating the reason for the change. Avoid placing blame with a statement such as, "After careful review of the film and a discussion with the radiologist, I believe the study indicates the following."

Date of Service

To eliminate any confusion that may arise during an audit, make sure the date located in the heading of the dictated report reflects the date of service rather than the date of dictation. Dictation and transcription dates are best located in the footer of the report.

Additional Studies

Based on findings from a routine x-ray exam, a radiologist may feel further studies are warranted. For example, a radiologist may elect to do tomograms on a patient whose chest x-ray revealed a mass. The documentation must indicate that the existence of the mass establishes the medical necessity for further studies. In such a situation, the radiologist is usually not required to check with the ordering physician before proceeding with additional studies.

Invasive/Interventional Radiology Procedures

Invasive or interventional radiology procedures are radiological studies accompanied by an invasive surgical procedure. Examples include venograms, angiograms, transcatheter abscess drainage, and x-ray guided biopsies.

The invasive procedure and the radiological study are generally performed by the same physician, but not always. Whether performed by one or two physicians, an interventional radiology procedure should be documented as thoroughly as a surgical procedure.

When an invasive radiology procedure is performed by two physicians, each physician should reference the other's involvement in the report. In the case of a kidney biopsy, a nephrologist may handle the invasive part including placement of the needle and obtaining tissue samples. The radiologist may be responsible for generating the x-rays, injecting the dye, and reading the film. Both physicians are responsible for a complete report of their portions of the procedure with a reference to the other physician's role.

Also, all invasive radiological procedures require consent, just like all invasive surgical procedures with significant risk. Consent is discussed in more detail in Chapter 4, Surgical Services.

The following is a suggested format for documenting invasive radiology procedures:

➤ Title of operation or procedure

➤ Clinical indication or reason for procedure

➤ Monitoring (optional)

➤ Sedation

➤ Detailed account of procedure

  • the procedure note must show performance of each procedure listed in the report heading

  • for vascular procedures, include the access route(s), each nonselective and selective vessel catheterized, and any deviation from normal anatomy

➤ Injections (including type and amount of contrast material)

➤ Findings

➤ Complications

➤ Post-procedure patient status

➤ Impression or short description of the findings

Problem Areas

The following are some common problems associated with documenting radiology procedures.

1. The report from the radiologist does not contain enough detail to warrant the CPT code billed.

   This problem often results from the dilemma created by the fact that physicians do not want to sift through a lot of information when reading radiology reports, but radiologists are supposed to document the exam in enough detail to justify reimbursement.

2. The order from the requesting physician does not provide enough history to establish a diagnosis.

   It is the ordering physician's responsibility to provide the radiologist with enough information to justify medical necessity.

3. The transcription contains inaccuracies due to misheard or misunderstood words.

   Radiologists must read transcriptions for accuracy before signing them. While this can be a cursory review, it is important in ensuring the appropriate diagnosis and treatment. There have been cases where the wrong kidney was removed because left appeared in the transcription instead of right. Physicians should always verify any information in the report that seems questionable.

4. Lag time exists between an exam and when the results are received by the physician.

   Because the patient is most likely already following a course of treatment, any unexpected results could mean a return visit for the patient and a change in the treatment. When opposite findings or unexpected results occur, the radiologist should call the physician with the findings. Once the written findings are received, the physician should check that they match the verbal findings communicated over the phone. Both the verbal and written communications should be recorded in the patient's chart.

Documenting Pathology and Laboratory Services

Many of the recommendations that apply to documenting radiology exams also pertain to pathology and laboratory tests. For instance, the physician must read and sign all pathology and laboratory reports to show that the information was received, reviewed, and taken into consideration in the overall managment of the patient's condition. These signed reports must then be incorporated into the patient's medical record. The actual report can be stored elsewhere, but a hard copy summary and interpretation of the pertinent findings must be included in the patient record. Exceptions to this rule are simple laboratory procedures performed in the office such as urinalysis, hematocrit, and latex agglutination. For these types of tests, recording the results in a dated laboratory test result log and in the patient's medical record is sufficient.

Like radiology exams, pathology and laboratory services must be medically necessary. As mentioned earlier in this chapter, it is important for the physician ordering the test to note in the patient record exactly how the findings were used in determining a diagnosis and selecting a treatment plan. In the event of an audit, this will demonstrate that the tests were necessary. All tests performed must be necessary and appropriate, and the results must be reviewed and actively used by the physician.

The most commonly performed pathology and laboratory services are conducted in the following way: A physician collects a specimen for testing and sends it to an outside lab. The lab conducts the ordered test and sends a report back to the physician.

Since most tests are computerized, the results are generally reported by a number value on a computer printout. However, it is not sufficient to merely copy that number value into the patient chart or attach the computer printout to the patient record. Instead, the physician must note the type of test, the methodology used, the normal range for the test, and then comment on whether the finding is abnormal or normal in relation to that range. Laboratories vary widely in the methods they use to analyze specimens. As a result, a normal range for a certain test at one lab may be an abnormal range for the same test at another lab. And while the physician who ordered the test may know the methods used by a particular lab, another physician may not know, and a misinterpretation could occur.

For example, a PO_2 blood gas test can be done by two different methods — electrode and manometry. Each method will report a different value and normal range. The best way to make this difference clear in the documentation is to simply state the following: "PO_2 measured by electrode resulted in _____. The normal range is _____."

When the lab report reveals an abnormal finding, the physician should circle and sign the abnormal result to indicate it was seen. The physician must also make sure to address the abnormality in the diagnosis and treatment plan.

Not all laboratory tests are handled by outside facilities. Routine tests, like urinalysis, are almost always handled by the clinic or practice. Documentation of these tests must include the date, the type of test, and the result. Because these tests are conducted in house, the physician can bill the service.

When the specimen is sent to an outside facility for testing, the lab performing the test should bill the service. However, it is appropriate for the physician to bill for the collection of the specimen if this service is provided by the physician's staff. When tests are performed in an outside laboratory, the name of the laboratory should be included in the report as well as in the patient's medical record.

Contents of a Lab Report

The lab report should contain the following elements:

➤ Patient name and identification number

➤ Name of laboratory

➤ Name of physician or practitioner ordering the test

➤ Date and time of specimen collection and date and time of receipt

➤ Reason for an unsatisfactory specimen

➤ Test or evaluation performed

➤ Result

➤ Date and time of report

Professional and Technical Components

Some pathology and laboratory procedures involve both a professional and technical component, such as invasive anatomical and surgical pathology services. These services require the physician to complete the procedure and collect the specimen. The lab then analyzes the specimen and gives the result to the physician who interprets it. An example of this type of test is a gastric intubation, which is a study of the stomach's chemicals. The physician performs the intubation and collects a sample. A laboratory technologist analyzes the sample and sends a report to the physician who interprets the result.

The majority of lab tests have only a technical component. These tests are performed by technicians at outside laboratory facilities, and the results are generally reported back to the physician on a computer printout. This automated type of reporting does not require interpretation on the part of the physician, so the physician cannot bill for it. The physician's evaluation of the significance of the laboratory finding is part of the overall patient Evaluation and Management (E/M) service.

Some pathology services involve only an interpretation and so only the professional component can be billed. An example of this type of service is an autopsy, which requires the physician to conduct the procedure and interpret the findings. There is no technical component.

Other Issues

When a lab test is ordered, the physician should document any relevant circumstances surrounding the specimen's collection that could affect the test results. For instance, if the patient has recently eaten, it can impact the results of a serum cholesterol test.

How a specimen was collected can also affect the results of a test. Documenting from what site the specimen was taken as well as the technique can lend important information to the findings. For example, blood gas drawn from an arterial line by a blood gas technician can provide different results than blood gas drawn percutaneously by a medical student.

Finally, both the date the specimen was collected and the date the actual test was performed should be recorded because some specimens change over time.

The physician or other person collecting the specimen should also note the following:

➤ Dimensions of specimen

➤ Source of specimen (where on body)

➤ Type of tissue

➤ Color of specimen

➤ Infectious agents

➤ Foreign bodies

➤ Drugs or antibiotics used by patient

The number of specimens and the number of containers should be recorded on the pathology report. If five specimens are received in one container, it is significantly different than if five specimens are received in five different containers. Labs must prepare each container as a new specimen.

6 Chart Assessment

The medical record serves a variety of purposes, all of which are important to the proper functioning of a medical practice in today's complicated healthcare environment. The medical record should detail information pertinent to the care of the patient, document the performance of billable services, and serve as a legal document that describes a course of treatment. Periodical audits help ensure that the record adequately serves these purposes.

Auditing a medical practice's charts can be an extremely valuable learning experience because it assesses the completeness of the medical record, the accuracy of the physician's documentation, and sources of lost revenue. An auditor, whether an employer of the practice or someone hired from the outside, examines the documentation to determine whether it adequately substantiates the service billed and identifies the medical necessity. Unless the quality of a practice's medical records is assessed on an ongoing basis, a physician or practice administrator may be unaware of incorrect or inappropriate documentation and coding practices, and areas of noncompliance with government and private payer guidelines.

Prior to performing a chart audit, identify specific goals. Chart audit objectives are generally divided into two main categories: revenue and compliance.

Revenue Objectives

An audit's revenue objectives involve examining coding practices for lost revenue due to the improper use of codes. This process can also reveal inappropriate billing for incorrectly high reimbursement—an open invitation for a payer audit. Revenue objectives are divided into the following subcategories.

Nonbilled Services

Compare the medical record to the billing to identify services that are documented in the medical record but for some reason are not coded. This is often caused by ineffective communication between the clinicians and the billing staff or a lack of knowledge on the part of the coders.

Overbilled or Underbilled Services

As with nonbilled services, the search for overbilled or underbilled services begins with comparing the chart documentation to the billed codes. All services, including evaluation and management and surgical procedures, should be explained in sufficient detail in the documentation to allow coders to choose the proper code.

Undocumented Services

A good audit will identify instances where codes are billed without proper supporting documentation. When a payer, either Medicare or a private insurance company, requests written proof of billed charges, the provider must be able to substantiate the service. The most commonly misplaced information is laboratory test results and x-ray reports.

Denied or Downcoded Services

Analyze those services that are denied or downcoded by payers to discover the cause of the denial. This information comes from comparing the billed services to the explanation of benefits (EOB) or explanation of Medicare benefits (EOMB) portion of the payer's statement.

Compliance Objectives

The second set of audit objectives involve evaluating the documentation for compliance with Medicare, Medicaid, and private payer standards. Not only are compliance issues important to the overall good management of patients, they are also important for expedient and accurate reimbursement.

Current Patient Data

Examine the patient information sheet to verify it collects all important information about the patient such as date of birth, address, nearest living relative, and insurance information. The patient information sheet should be updated regularly.

Request that patients with insurance sign an assignment-of-benefits form to ensure direct payment of insurance benefits to the provider. Update this record yearly. Medicare offers a lifetime signature form which must also be kept on file by the provider.

Physician Signatures

A thorough audit will verify that all services and procedures provided to a patient are signed by the physician. The signature of the physician acknowledges that he or she has performed or supervised the service or procedure. An unsigned entry in a medical record may be viewed by an insurance payer as nonperformance of that service.

Chart entries that are not in the physician's handwriting should be countersigned by the attending physician. This includes medical services performed by a nurse or telephone conversations between patients and staff members.

Signed Consent Forms

The medical record of each patient that undergoes a procedure involving significant risk should contain a written consent form. Always obtain consent before conducting an invasive procedure. The consent should state that the patient has been informed about the procedure, its risks and benefits, and the alternatives. It should also indicate the patient understood the issues discussed and gave consent to treatment. This information may be kept in a separate section or accompany the documentation of the procedure.

Medicare Limitation of Liability

The government has published a list of services it classifies as medically unnecessary for the Medicare program. When providing these services to a medicare beneficiary, obtain a signed waiver known as the limitation of liability. This notification informs the patient in advance that the services he or she seeks may be denied, and he or she is responsible to pay the bill.

Insurance Forms

An auditor should check claim forms, whether submitted electronically or by hard copy, to see that they are completed correctly. Include all pertinent dates and diagnostic and procedural coding information necessary for insurance payers to generate reimbursement.

Performing the Chart Audit

The initial steps of performing a chart audit include assembling the necessary materials for the analysis and comparing the documentation to the procedural and diagnostic codes. The auditor should have a list of the objectives and keep a tally of various findings.

Gather Reference Materials

The auditor must use current CPT and ICD-9 coding books as well as the previous year's edition of each book. A HCPCS Level II book will be required when reviewing supplies and equipment billed to Medicare.

Select Charts to be Reviewed

Start by reviewing 10 charts for each physician to get a good sample of each physician's services. Another method is to target specific services. In either case, the charts selected should contain examples of services performed by each physician. Since the focus should be on current coding, review only those services less than one year old.

Obtain Insurance Information

Gather insurance information, either copies of submitted HCFA-1500 forms or computerized insurance data, for each date of service assessed. Review the insurance information submitted for completeness.

Obtain EOBs and EOMBs

Reviewing the explanation of benefits (EOBs) or explanation of Medicare benefits (EOMBs) statements provided by payers can be a valuable way for providers to discover unacceptable code use or incorrect sequencing of codes. When a certain service results in consistent denial or substantial reduction in payment by more than one payer, the coding practice should be analyzed and corrected. This review may reveal a claim form with codes that are transposed, outdated, or improperly sequenced.

The EOB and EOMB statements can provide a method to track payers' usual, reasonable, and customary (UCR) amounts. Compare the UCRs of different insurance companies for insight into keeping fees current and in line with the market.

Unfortunately, EOBs and EOMBs can be difficult to read because each payer may have its own format. Whenever possible, ask the insurance payer to provide specific information or break down the charges paid. Ideally, the explanation of the payment provided by the payer identifies the date of service being reimbursed, the charges submitted, the allowed payment determined by the payer, and whether the patient's deductible is subtracted from the payment made to the payer.

Develop a Tally Sheet

The auditor will need a form to record the frequency of correct and incorrect coding and documentation errors.

The following is an overview of information that should be recorded on the tally sheet:

➤ Patient chart number and physician name
➤ Date of service
➤ Correct CPT codes
➤ Incorrect CPT codes

➤ Corrected CPT codes

➤ CPT codes coded but not documented

➤ CPT codes documented but not coded

➤ Correct ICD-9 codes

➤ Incorrect ICD-9

➤ Corrected ICD-9

➤ ICD-9 codes coded but not documented

➤ ICD-9 codes documented but not coded

➤ Patient's consent

➤ Physician's signature

➤ Patient's signature (for release of medical information and assignment of benefits)

➤ Whether the patient has Medicare or non-Medicare insurance

At the completion of the chart audit, total and analyze the tally sheets to determine practices that need attention as well as practices that are being performed well. Develop percentages in the following areas:

➤ Correct use of CPT codes

- levels of service

- diagnostic procedures

- surgical codes

➤ Incorrect use of CPT codes

- inadequate documentation

- fragmented billing

➤ Correct use of ICD-9 codes

➤ Incorrect use of ICD-9 codes

- inadequate documentation

- incomplete coding

- incorrect codes

➤ Appropriate physician signatures

➤ Appropriate patient signatures

**Take Action Based
on Findings**

A chart audit is a useless exercise if no action is taken on the findings, even if that action is just an acknowledgement that the documentation, coding, and billing practices are acceptable. The physicians and the practice administrator should review the ratio of correct and incorrect coding as well as compliance and noncompliance issues. Areas of incomplete or inaccurate documentation can be identified and corrective action taken. Establish a time frame to make needed changes based on the physicians' or practice administrator's determination of the issues that require immediate attention and those that can wait for long-term revision and implementation.

7 Legal Issues

Professional liability claims against healthcare providers have increased significantly during recent years in both the number of claims and the average payment for a judgment or settlement. Because of these increases, the insurance industry has substantially increased the cost of medical malpractice insurance. According to a comprehensive study on medical malpractice by researchers at Harvard University, the average physician in New York state paid $360 for liability coverage in 1949. In 1965, 16 years later, the cost of the same coverage was just $1,000. But by 1975 it leaped to $7,300, and by the end of the 1980s, the average cost of reasonably full insurance protection was near $40,000, which is more than 100 times the price of the same protection four decades earlier. The study also notes that in higher risk specialties, such as neurosurgery, orthopedic surgery, and obstetrics, annual premiums may reach levels as high as $150,000 to $200,000 a year in larger cities like New York. Even in states where insurance costs are at or near the national average of roughly $15,000 a year per physician, the trend is toward higher premium rates.

When looking at malpractice claims frequency, measured by the number of claims per physician per year, the Harvard study found that the number rose from just over one claim per 100 physicians per year in the late 1950s to well over 10 claims per 100 physicians in the mid 1980s. At the same time, the average payment made on successful claims rose from $40,000 in 1970 to nearly $150,000 by the end of the 1980s. Some cases, however, render much higher awards. The Harvard researchers state that each year at least one medical malpractice case ranks among the largest jury awards for that year in the entire U.S. legal system: a $52 million verdict in Houston in 1988, a $78 million award in Chicago in 1990, and a $127 million award in Illinois in 1991.

The effect of increased insurance premiums and increased claims is increased healthcare costs, both through the healthcare providers passing the cost of premiums to the patient and through the providers practicing defensive medicine because a patient may be viewed as a potential adversary in a lawsuit. Further, certain healthcare providers may be discouraged from continuing to provide services because of the high cost and possible unavailability of malpractice insurance.

In New York state, this is already a reality. *OBG Management,* in its July 1993 issue, reported that 16 percent of New York state's obstetric care providers have stopped practicing because of liability. In New York, 88.5 percent of the American College of Obstetrics and Gynecology fellows have been sued at least once, and almost 48 percent have been sued four or more times. The number of suits has increased 387 percent since 1980. *OBG Management* states that if that rate continues, physicians practicing obstetrics in New York state can expect to be sued at least four times.

Claims against healthcare providers frequently fall within an identifiable pattern. By identifying these patterns and linking them to problem areas encountered in practice, risk management guidelines can be established to prevent claims from arising. Claims against providers frequently occur in the areas of documentation and inadequate record keeping, adverse results from medical treatment, lack of informed consent, referrals and abandonment, breach of confidentiality, and deficiencies in the interaction between patients and healthcare providers and their staffs.

Because documentation is involved in many of these areas, attention to careful documentation practices can help to improve patient care and may serve to relieve the anxiety often felt by healthcare providers working in a difficult medical-legal climate. Accurate and complete documentation can also increase a provider's chances of a positive outcome once involved in a claim.

Medical–Legal Terms

Before detailing the malpractice problem areas, this chapter will describe some of the most common medical-legal terms associated with professional liability claims.

Malpractice or Professional Negligence

A malpractice action against a healthcare provider includes any action against a healthcare provider, whether in contract, tort, breach of warranty, wrongful death or otherwise, based on alleged personal injuries relating to or arising out of healthcare rendered or that should have been rendered by the healthcare provider.

A healthcare provider is generally defined as any person, partnership, association, corporation, or other facility or institution that causes to be rendered or who renders healthcare or professional services. Examples include hospitals, physicians, nurses, or agents of any of the above acting in the course and scope of their employment.

Malpractice is a form of negligence. Negligence is usually defined as the omission to do something that a reasonable person, guided by the ordinary considerations that ordinarily regulate human affairs, would do; or doing something that a reasonable and prudent person would not do. Negligence is based on the breach of a duty on the part of one person to exercise care to protect another against injury. Negligence is a failure to observe a legal duty, and where there is no duty, no legal liability can arise.

Four elements must be established to prove negligence on the part of a healthcare provider.

Patient-Provider Relationship
When a healthcare provider agrees or begins to care for a patient, this relationship is created. Once the relationship is established, a legal duty exists to employ the required knowledge, skill, and care in treatment that would ordinarily be possessed by other members of the profession.

Breach of Duty
When a healthcare provider fails to possess and exercise the knowledge and care ordinarily used by other reasonable practitioners under the same or similar circumstances, then the healthcare provider has violated the standard of care and has breached the duty owed to the patient. The term "standard of care" relates to the healthcare provider's duty to exercise that degree of skill and learning ordinarily possessed and exercised, under similar circumstances, by other practitioners in the field of practice. Whether a strict locality, similar community, or national standard is applied will depend on the established law within each jurisdiction. The majority of states apply the same or similar community standard to measure the duty of care. However, for nationally trained and board certified healthcare providers, a higher national standard of care may be used.

Expert medical testimony is usually required to establish the standard of care and a deviation from the standard on the part of the healthcare provider. Expert medical testimony is required because most jury members lack the medical training necessary to determine appropriate medical procedure. However, in some instances, expert testimony is not required if it is deemed within the common knowledge. The term "res ipsa loquitur," which literally means the thing speaks for itself, permits an inference of negligence on the basis of circumstantial evidence. For example, a sponge or scissors left in the abdomen following surgery often requires no expert testimony because everyone realizes such an event should not occur with appropriate medical care.

Causation

A patient, in making a professional liability claim against a healthcare provider, must establish a causal connection or relationship between the act or omission of the healthcare provider and the injury that resulted. This is commonly known as proximate cause.

Damages

The patient making a claim must prove that the damage complained of was caused or incurred by the healthcare provider's malpractice, negligence, or breach of the standard of care. Damages frequently include past and future medical expenses, pain and suffering, and claims for impairment or disability.

Vicarious Liability—Let the Master Pay

Even though a healthcare provider such as a physician may not have personally been negligent in the treatment, the physician may bear liability exposure for the wrongful acts of others he or she employs. This is referred to as "vicarious liability" or "respondeat superior," and is based on the principle that the master should pay or be held responsible for the wrongful acts of the people who work for or are under his or her control and supervision. Thus, the most careful physician can face significant liability exposure for improperly trained staff, inadequate documentation, and overall inefficient risk management practices in the office.

Patient Records and Documentation

A separate medical record should be kept for each patient. This file should contain the patient's health history and updates; copies of any signed consent forms and entries documenting discussions on consent; the results of laboratory studies and other diagnostic tests; a treatment summary for each office visit; a prescription record; and a summary of telephone conversations with the patient. It should also include a record of scheduled appointments and missed appointments, referral notations or consultations concerning other healthcare providers, and laboratory and x-ray interpretations.

If a patient is involved in litigation, properly preserving the medical chart, prescription record, results of diagnostic tests, and billing ledger is essential. Most hospitals handle patient charts in litigation by placing them in a different location under lock and key for protection and preservation. This practice is also recommended in an office or clinic setting.

Once a professional liability claim is filed against a healthcare provider, correspondence with the insurance carrier and with the defense attorney should be kept in a separate location from the treatment record. These materials are afforded legal protection against disclosure and should not be readily volunteered as part of the patient's treatment record. Incident reports and peer review information are also often afforded legal protection from disclosure and are best kept separate from the actual patient treatment chart as well.

When documenting patient visits, the SOAP (subjective, objective, assessment and plan) approach is recommended because it standardizes the way physicians record patient visits. The SOAP method provides an excellent format for describing the patient's subjective complaints, the physician's objective findings and assessment, and the treatment plan. See Chapter 3, Evaluation and Management Services, for a more detailed description of the SOAP format.

In addition, the healthcare provider should keep copies of all prescriptions and clearly document medications being taken by the patient. Using standardized abbreviations is also a helpful documentation practice.

Patient medical records should be kept for long periods of time. It is difficult to give an exact time line for record retention because statutes of limitations differ among states and jurisdictions. Also, in the case of minors, even longer time periods must be observed because in many states the statute of limitations does not even begin until the minor reaches the age of majority. This means that claims can be brought a number of years after the care was rendered, making long-term record retention necessary.

Alterations

Records should never be altered or changed at any time after a lawsuit is filed. Defense lawyers would much rather defend an incomplete or nonexistent record than one that has been fraudulently altered. The ability of experts to detect alterations has become extremely advanced. In fact, handwriting experts are frequently retained by lawyers in professional liability cases to examine the patient record and determine if late or fraudulent alterations have been made. A case that may otherwise be defendable may be lost due to a fraudulent change in the patient's record.

George Throckmorton, the nationally known handwriting expert who declared the Howard Hughes will a forgery, is frequently called on to determine whether medical treatment records have been altered. Throckmorton reports that a large number of medical records that end up in medical malpractice litigation have been significantly altered.

In some cases, however, handwriting experts establish that the record was not altered. For example, an emergency room physician was named in a claim for wrongful death of a 36-year-old walk-in patient. The patient refused to be admitted after examination even though the physician attempted to convince him it was necessary. The physician did not have the patient sign an AMA (against medical advice) discharge acknowledgment form before leaving the hospital. Instead the physician wrote these five words in the treatment record: "Patient refuses to be admitted." The patient returned to the car and told his wife the hospital would not admit him. Five hours later he died in bed at home. His spouse filed a malpractice action against the physician and hospital for failure to properly diagnose, admit, and treat her husband. Her attorney believed the chart entry was made after the fact by the physician and subpoenaed the original record for expert review by Throckmorton. The expert determined the entry was made at the time by the physician. The case was dismissed.

From a medical malpractice perspective, it is extremely important to maintain and preserve accurate and unaltered treatment records. Cases that could otherwise be successfully defended are often settled when alterations were made by the provider. In spite of even good intentions on the part of the healthcare provider in altering a record, judges and juries lose all confidence in the credibility of the provider in the face of such alterations.

If an alteration is warranted and the patient record is not involved in a lawsuit, the entry can be changed as long as several guidelines are followed. The error should never be corrected using "white out" or by erasure. It is best to draw a single line through the incorrect entry so that it is still readable, then write the correct entry into the record. Also sign and date the change and indicate why it was necessary. Refer to Chapter 1, Basic Documentation, for more information on making changes to the patient record.

Health Histories

Many claims are brought against healthcare providers for failure to obtain an adequate medical history to assist in the diagnosis or treatment of the patient's condition. Healthcare providers should record and maintain a proper medical history for each patient. There are many forms available for recording a patient's medical history, and whatever form is used should be tailored to the specific needs of the practice's specialty. Usually the office staff handles having the patient complete these forms and updating them. The health histories should be consistently completed, dated and signed by the patient, and updated on a regular basis.

Health histories should gather information about all health problems that may impact the evaluation of the risks involved in a contemplated medical procedure or treatment plan. The completed health history in the patient's file should make the provider aware of any hazards the patient may present and of any negative effects that treatment may produce in a given patient. The completed health history should be discussed with the patient prior to the start of any procedure. Responses that indicate a patient has symptoms reflecting underlying medical problems should prompt additional questions. Review of the form and discussion with the patient should generally be handled by the physician.

Releasing Medical Records

The issue of who owns the medical record, whether the healthcare provider or the patient, has been debated for decades. It is generally recognized that a healthcare provider has the right to maintain and preserve the patient record, but the patient has a right of access to the record and to obtain copies upon appropriate request. Because of the physician/patient privilege, it is important to maintain confidentiality concerning the patient's treatment and records reflecting that treatment. A medical release should be obtained from a patient before releasing records to third persons. A healthcare provider may charge reasonable photocopy or x-ray duplication fees for reproducing records. The amount that can be charged may be regulated within the state or jurisdiction in which the provider practices.

A number of states require a written authorization before records can be released to third persons. These authorizations must be signed and acknowledged by the patient before a notary public; or in the case of a minor, by a parent or guardian; or in the case of a deceased patient, by the personal representative or an heir. Original x-rays and records in litigated matters should not be released in the absence of a subpoena or court order, and even then the healthcare provider may want to consult with legal counsel before such release.

The amount of time records should be kept depends on the laws of the jurisdiction and the type of practice. Statutes of limitations vary widely around the country and are mainly aimed at containing the number of claims entering the litigation process. Records must obviously be preserved beyond the time period in which a professional liability claim can be filed. On the average this time period is seven to eight years. Where minors are concerned, records must be kept much longer than adult medical records. Many states do not begin the statute of limitations until a minor reaches the age of majority. Pediatricians and obstetricians are therefore better off paying for storage and keeping their records longer than to risk destroying a record before the statute of limitations has expired.

Informed Consent

The relationship between a healthcare provider and a patient is a consensual one, and in the absence of an emergency or unanticipated condition, a healthcare provider must first obtain consent before treating or operating on the patient. If a patient who is capable of exercising free judgment refuses to allow treatment then accuses the healthcare provider of negligence by not providing treatment, the provider can use the refusal as a defense. However, the provider must be able to prove the refusal in the documentation.

The law generally presumes that an individual is competent and capable of managing his or her own affairs, and a healthcare provider is entitled to rely upon that presumption until the contrary is shown. When dealing with minor children, consent should be obtained from the child's parents or guardian.

Consent to medical treatment may handled in several ways. The patient may express consent by oral agreement or by signing a formal written permission. Also, the patient may give implied consent through conduct such as voluntary submission to the operation or by failure to object. Consent for treatment of a minor child is often implied from the fact that the adult relatives of the child are present.

The nature and extent of the consent depends on the medical problem as well as on the patient. Many basic treatment procedures are within the ordinary realm of knowledge and understanding of the patient and, therefore, consent to treatment is most often implied. Most courts have found that substantial and significant risks must be disclosed to a patient, but remote risks need not be.

As far as what information must be disclosed, the standard is generally measured from the physician's viewpoint (reasonable physician's standard). These jurisdictions hold that the duty is measured by professional medical standards on what a reasonable and prudent physician would disclose under the same or similar circumstances. Thus, expert testimony is required to establish the duty of disclosure and any departure from the standard.

A minority of jurisdictions have measured the duty from the patient's viewpoint (reasonable patient standard). In these jurisdictions, the healthcare provider must disclose information about the treatment which a reasonable patient would deem material to his or her decision.

A healthcare provider is not responsible for failing to disclose risks not reasonably foreseeable and not inherent to the procedure. A physician need not disclose risks known to the patient or risks that are so obvious that knowledge can be presumed. Usually a description of the procedure, the alternatives, and the substantial and serious risks is deemed sufficient.

Written Consent Forms

Written consent forms are often used because they provide easy proof in a subsequent dispute. These forms often state that the patient has been informed of the possible risks of the procedure and that consent has been given to treatment. Even a general consent of this type when signed by a patient can be effective in defending a claim for lack of informed consent. For example, many states have statutes that provide a legal presumption in favor of the healthcare provider that consent was informed where a patient has signed a written consent. An attorney should be consulted concerning drafting a written consent form to comply with the legal requirement of the state in which the provider practices.

Documenting Referrals and Avoiding Abandonment

Many professional liability claims allege failure to refer the patient to a specialist for medical treatment in a timely manner. A general practitioner is usually allowed by license to perform broad medical treatment, but when treating a patient in a highly specialized area, that physician will likely be held to the higher standard of care expected of a specialist. By referring a patient to a specialist in a timely manner, many malpractice claims can be avoided and better quality healthcare maintained. A patient referral should be considered when a second opinion is requested or when there is a general discomfort and lack of experience with the proposed treatment.

Good communication is essential when referring a patient to another physician. The physician should be contacted concerning the ability to treat the patient. The name, address, and phone number of the physician should be clearly communicated to the patient. It is often a good idea to provide the patient with a choice of physicians. Giving the patient only one name could possibly involve some overlapping liability should a claim arise with the second physician. A description of what is expected of the physician will also avoid miscommunication. Upon proper release by the patient, the prior treatment record should be forwarded to the new physician. The treatment chart should then document the referral and the reason for the referral.

Abandonment claims are occasionally made against healthcare providers who fail to appropriately terminate the healthcare provider/patient relationship. It is much easier to avoid the relationship than to get out of the relationship once established. Thus, being more selective before treatment can avoid many uncomfortable treatment situations that may lead to an abandonment claim.

If the patient is terminating the relationship, the physician should clearly document that in the chart. It is helpful to send a letter to the patient outlining unfinished treatments and future treatment recommendations. If the healthcare provider is terminating the relationship, then it should be done at a time that will not jeopardize the patient's care, and the patient should be allowed an appropriate period of time in which to obtain other healthcare.

Recommendations for obtaining other healthcare are helpful, and a summary of the patient's needed care should be provided. By sending this letter via certified mail, a future claim contending lack of receipt of the termination letter can be avoided.

In Conclusion

The best way to avoid a professional liability claim is to provide quality healthcare and to carefully and completely document that care and preserve the record. But all claims cannot be avoided because many factors are beyond the control of the healthcare provider. A better understanding of the medical-legal climate and of the problem areas of practice outlined above will assist in reducing or preventing many of the types of claims frequently encountered.

August 1993

David H. Epperson, Attorney at Law
Dave Epperson, of Hanson, Epperson & Smith in Salt Lake City, Utah, specializes in medical malpractice litigation and professional liability defense.

Index

Appendix A: Common Acronyms and Abbreviations

A	assessment	**Dx**	diagnosis
@	at	**ECG**	electrocardiogram
a.c.	before eating	**EKG**	electrocardiogram
BS	breath sounds/bowel sounds	**E/M**	evaluation and management
bx	biopsy	**EOM**	extraocular motion
c̄	with	**EOMI**	extraocular motion intact
CC	chief complaint	**ET**	endotracheal
cm	centimeter	**Fx**	fracture
cm²	square centimeters	**HMS**	hepatosplenomegaly
CN	cranial nerves	**HPI**	history of present illness
D	day	**ht**	height
Disp	disposition	**HTN**	hypertension
DOB	date of birth	**Hx**	history
Dsg	dressing	**ICS**	intercostal space
DTRs	deep tendon reflexes	**IV**	intravenous

(L)	left	**ROS**	review of systems
lb	pound	**RRR**	regular rate and rhythm
LE	lower extremity	**s**	without
LMP	last menstrual period	**SOB**	shortness of breath
MCL	midclavicular line	**Sx**	sign/symptom
NKMA	no known medical allergies	**TBSA**	total body surface area
OD	right eye	**TM**	tympanic membrane
OS	left eye	**Tx**	treatment
p̄	after	**UE**	upper extremity
P	plan	**WNL**	within normal limits
p.c.	after eating	**Wt**	weight
PE	physical examination	**x̄**	except
PMHx	past medical history	**Y-O**	year-old
PMI	point of maximum intensity	♀	female
PO	by mouth	♂	male
PCN	penicillin		
PR	per rectum		
PRN	as needed for		
Pt	patient		
PTA	prior to admission		
Q	every		
QID	four times daily		
(R)	right		
R/O	rule out		
ROM	range of motion		

Other References

The following is a list of publications on acronyms and abbreviations:

Delong, Marilyn Fuller. *Medical Acronyms & Abbreviations.* Oradell, NJ: Medical Economics Books, 1985.

Hamilton, Betty; Guidos, Barbara, editors. *MASA: Medical Acronyms, Symbols & Abbreviations, 2nd Edition.* New York, NY: Neal-Schuman Publishers, Inc., 1988.

Sloane, Sheila B. *Medical Abbreviations and Eponyms.* Philadelphia, PA: W.B. Saunders Co., 1985.

Appendix B: Forms

This appendix contains forms to help you develop sound documentation practices. The forms are perforated so they can be removed easily. You are encouraged to photocopy and use these forms or develop similar forms customized for your office.